Y
WIL   Williamson, Denise
       River of danger

GOD'S TOUGH GUYS

Stephen, *the First Martyr*
Samuel Kirkland, *Missionary to the Senecas*
St. Vincent de Paul, *Priest and Pirate Captive*
Eric Liddell, *Olympic Star*

GOD'S TOUGH GUYS

RIVER OF DANGER

A Story of Samuel Kirkland

DENISE WILLIAMSON

Illustrated by JOE BODDY

Wolgemuth & Hyatt, Publishers, Inc.
Brentwood, Tennessee

to
Gary
my lifelong friend

RIVER OF DANGER

Text © 1990 by Denise J. Williamson

Illustrations © 1990 by March Media, Inc.

Wolgemuth & Hyatt, Publishers, Inc.

1749 Mallory Lane, Brentwood, Tennessee 37027

Book Development by March Media, Inc., Brentwood, Tennessee

First Edition September 1990

PRINTED IN THE UNITED STATES OF AMERICA

Library of Congress Cataloging-in-Publication Data

Williamson, Denise J., 1954-
    River of danger / Denise Williamson.
        p. cm. — (God's tough guys)
    Summary: While spying on Samuel Kirkland, the first missionary to the Seneca Indians, Young-Wolf learns the meaning of friendship and bravery from his white-skinned brother during a life-threatening winter.
    ISBN 1-56121-027-7
    1. Kirkland, Samuel, 1741-1808—Juvenile fiction. 2. Seneca Indians—Juvenile fiction. [1. Kirkland, Samuel, 1741-1808- -Fiction. 2. Missionaries—Fiction. 3. Seneca Indians—Fiction. 4. Indians of North America—Fiction. 5. Christian life—Fiction.] I. Title. II. Series: Williamson, Denise J., 1954- God's tough guys.
PZ7.W6714R1 1990
[Fic]—dc20
                          90-43925
                          CIP
                          AC

CONTENTS

1

THE KNIFE RACE

Young-Wolf feared he would drown in the snow. Bear-Lad's hands pressed his head back into the drifts. His knees dug deep into Young-Wolf's ribs.

Young-Wolf spit ice into the face of his opponent. He wagged his head until his vision cleared. He would not give in to the strongest boy wrestler in Ganundasaga.

Above him, a cluster of younger boys watched the contest. Their wide eyes told Young-Wolf that he might have a chance. His arms became black snakes, squeezing life from their prey. His toes were moles, finding firm ground without sight. A moment later he flipped Bear-Lad. The boy landed like an overturned box turtle, clawing air that was thick with falling snow.

Young-Wolf sat up on his heels. Whooping for victory, he tossed back his head and felt snowflakes burst on his tongue. The little boys hooted their approval. In the flurry, none of them saw Ganundasaga's chief warrior walk up.

"Young-Wolf, I wish to talk," the warrior said as snow fell onto his bare chest and shoulders. Except for

two feathers tied to his long black scalp lock, he wore nothing more than a fringed knee-length kilt, a beaded belt, moccasins, and snowshoes.

Young-Wolf straightened his deerskin shirt as he stood. "It is good to see you, Captain." He chose the war leader's favored title.

"You and your brother from the Bear Clan show strength," the warrior observed. "Now if either or both of you prove to be daring as well, I might find room for you among the men who follow me."

Bear-Lad scrambled to his feet beside Young-Wolf. They traded excited glances. Their unplanned tussle had won them Captain's attention. The other boys listened with envy as one of the Seneca nation's bravest war captains continued his words.

"Strength is not courage," Captain said. "The young hawk in the nest may be strong enough—but still too afraid—to fly."

Young-Wolf's cheek muscle twitched. Words pressed on his tongue, but he was silent. To interrupt was a mark of disrespect. But Bear-Lad spoke.

"We can throw an axe to the center of a target and take a partridge on the wing with either a gun or a bow. Whatever challenge you put before us, Captain, we will do."

"Ho-hoo, brother!" Captain said, his eyebrows rising. "Then wade the river at the mouth of Lake Ganundasaga. Run north as far as the first great Hemlock Stand. Swim the deep water back, and return to the village by way of the Six-Nations Trail."

Bear-Lad's eyes widened as his shoulders fell.

9

Captain looked at Young-Wolf. "And you, Wolf-clan brother, are you as timid as Bear-Lad?"

Young-Wolf looked at his lanky friend, two summers older and a head taller than he. Then he spoke the only words that would win Captain's approval. "Not only will we run," he said. "We will *race* to see who's faster."

The scar across Captain's cheek and chin deepened as he smiled. "I like you, Young-Wolf. It is good to see that hardship and cold do not bring you fear." The warrior pulled a knife from the holder on his belt.

"I will give this to the boy who returns to Ganundasaga first," he said.

Young-Wolf eyed it cautiously.

"You disapprove?" Captain asked.

"I do not crave things made by white men," Young-Wolf said, his hand coming to rest on the ancient stone knife hanging from his own belt. "I race to show my strength as a Seneca. I race because I am the brother of Six Nations, united and proud."

Captain chuckled. "Again you speak bravely and well. I will remember your good words."

"He speaks, but can he race?" Bear-Lad challenged. With that he had his snowshoes on. He started toward the river.

Young-Wolf grabbed his own snowshoes hanging in the spicebushes and pushed his toes under the laces. He raced after Bear-Lad, staying close enough to hear the swish of his clan-brother's feet through the snow.

"Will you really swim the river?" Bear-Lad panted over his shoulder as they pushed on.

Young-Wolf didn't answer. He didn't know.

Where the river ran out from Lake Ganundasaga they reached the shallow fording place. On the shore they threw themselves down and pulled off their snowshoes. Young-Wolf jumped in first, holding his snowshoes high above his head. The icy water's teeth chewed up to his knees.

Bear-Lad worked to keep beside him. His teeth chattered, his tongue complained. "Water this cold should be stiff!" he said. "I'm sure not *swimming* back through this. Let's go farther upriver than Captain wants us to. There's another easy crossing there—the one that's used by travelers who walk toward the sunset from the Cayuga towns."

Young-Wolf reached the shore. He pushed his wet feet to the webbing of his snowshoe frames.

"Well, what do you say?" Bear-Lad urged as he fixed his own snowshoes. "Take the easy crossing? Right?"

Young-Wolf pressed on, unwilling to speak. Twelve springs ago his mother had carried him from the forest birthing-hut where he had taken his first breaths. It was time for him to swim the river and prove to Captain that he was as brave as a Seneca man.

"You won't speak," Bear-Lad fretted. "So, we race! And I'll beat you. I know you want that English knife as much as I do!" He jabbed Young-Wolf in the back and passed him. Young-Wolf let him go. He knew it would tire his Bear-clan brother to break a new trail through the open woods.

The Ganundasaga River stayed at Young-Wolf's left hand like a shiny black ribbon unraveled on bolts of white man's flannel. Young-Wolf kept his eye on it as he raced. Tall naked trees looked down on him. Laurel and huckleberry whispered as his moving arms stirred their branches. After a long hard journey, he saw what he was looking for. Across the deep water, the Six-Nations Trail was in view.

Bear-Lad was out of sight by now. Young-Wolf paused beneath the hemlocks to seek the wisdom in their sighing. He talked to them in short pants as he caught his breath. "You hold the sunlight in your arms. You keep the warmth of it from the river. I walk among you to see if you have saved a bridge for me."

Pulling off his snowshoes, he skidded down the bank. He saw just what he had imagined—a frozen trail of ice spanned the dark river. Young-Wolf gave thanks to the forest as he threw his snowshoes across his back. He shuffled out onto the frozen strip that crossed the gurgling waters. The Six-Nations Trail would soon meet him on the other side. Without a doubt now, he'd beat his Bear-clan brother.

Suddenly the bridge of ice cracked like a gun blast. It tossed Young-Wolf into water that burned with cold. He bit his lip and forced himself to swim. *The shore. . . . The shore. . . .* He made the sounds of swirling water cheer him on.

But the black river worked its awful magic, changing his arms and legs to stone. "I drown!" he cried as his long hair tangled in the currents.

Something with the grip of iron caught his chin. He rolled his eyes in fear and saw Captain's face above his own. Young-Wolf tried to scream. Headless warriors haunted the forest. That Captain's own face should appear while he was dying was more than he could bear.

He moaned when sharp roots on the riverbank scraped his back and legs. Fingers pressed against his lips to silence him. Young-Wolf pushed himself up to vomit out the evil water. He rocked forward in the waist-deep snow and collapsed in its softness.

His senses returned. *The race. . . . The knife. . . . The trail.* He scrambled to his feet. Below him, the river held its only prize—his snowshoes, which floated with the broken ice. Young-Wolf turned his back on them. He waded the snow to the trail. The feet of many travelers had beaten a pathway there. Once his wind returned, he found it easy enough to race on moccasins toward home.

He smelled the cooking fires of Ganundasaga. The women's cornfields, distant cabins, and twin two-story blockhouses of his village came into view.

"Ha-ga! Little-Brother!"

Young-Wolf jumped in surprise. Two Seneca scouts were sitting by the trail ahead.

"You wait for permission to enter our village?" Young-Wolf asked them on the run. These were the rules of travel: Visitors must be escorted into town by a messenger who served Chief Old-Smoke, Young-Wolf's grandfather.

The men nodded while continuing to smoke their pipes. "We and the white man we bring," they called after him.

Their words made Young-Wolf reel back. "What white man?" he snapped.

The older scout pointed across the trail to the young, thin paleface who sat with bare legs stretched lengthwise on a fallen log. His short straight hair was almost as dark as an Indian's, but his hands and face were as fair as dead beech leaves. The Indian leggings he wore had been slit and rolled to his knees to make room for his swollen limbs and ankles.

"His skin is the color of death!" Young-Wolf said, turning away in disgust. "And his legs! They are no more use for walking than two filled corn sacks."

The older scout nodded in agreement. "The man is new to snowshoes. He has suffered this way since our second day out from Johnson Hall. Yet he has walked from the middle of the Cold Moon until now—twenty-one days—without complaining."

"And you want to take him into Ganundasaga?" Young-Wolf squinted. Any white man was unwelcome in his eyes. But this one should never be allowed closer than the cropfields.

"We have a wampum belt from Sir William Johnson himself that tells the purpose of his coming." The younger scout held out some of his supplies. "Here, help us. He has a small pack and two blankets to carry."

"Never!" Young-Wolf threw his hands behind his back.

The younger scout ignored Young-Wolf's arrogance, but the older scout stood up to him. "I can understand your feelings, Ha-ga, but truly this man Samuel-Kirkland does not deserve your sharp word."

Young-Wolf glared at him. "Any white ma—" His throat froze. Bear-Lad was racing past him on the trail!

"You won't win now!" the other boy sang out, though his face dripped with sweat and his eyes bulged.

"You!!!" Young-Wolf screamed, and he went after him. He needed his snowshoes now to push through the snowy cornfields as Bear-Lad did. He yowled for

14

strength, but the river had eaten too much of his energy. Ahead, half of the village—perhaps two hundred and fifty spectators—lined the edge of the town to watch them finish the race.

Bear-Lad, more than two strides in the lead, pushed through the crowd, and Captain silently laid the knife into his quivering hand.

Young-Wolf finished the race with his head high, but his heart bowed down. Bear-Lad was panting beside him, with the knife raised over their heads. "This could have been yours." He laughed. "But you stopped for a white man on the trail."

"I did not!" Young-Wolf screamed angrily. But it was useless to argue.

In the fields, the two agile scouts broke trail for the lame man who set his face toward town. Chief Old-Smoke's messenger, who had been sent out to them, glided around them and back toward Ganundasaga like a low-flying hawk.

"So, it is true!" a little girl shouted. "Here comes that white man who stopped Young-Wolf on the path."

Young-Wolf dropped his head to his chest and wearily started home. He felt Captain follow him through the mud-marked snows that framed the log and bark-sided cabins.

"Young-Wolf," Captain said, finally stopping him at a cooking fire that had been abandoned for the excitement at the edge of town.

Young-Wolf faced the disapproval in Captain's eyes. "I listen, Captain."

"Your tongue speaks one thing, your actions another," Captain said. "Today you had the spirit of a warrior. But somewhere it left you on the trail. You return in defeat—beaten by a white man's limping gait?"

"It was the scout who slowed me down, not the white man," Young-Wolf braved, his kettle of anger boiling. "Is it a sign of weakness that I stopped for him?"

"I favored you. That is why I saved you from the waters. But still you lost—the knife, the race, the challenge. My followers are not losers, Ha-ga. If you want my respect, you must earn it."

"But I spoke for you," Young-Wolf raged. "I questioned why the scouts would bring this man to town, just as you would have done. And if I had been a warrior with a tomahawk in his belt, I could have done more than talk." He raised a fist to give power to his words.

Captain shook his head. "I doubt that. Certainly Chief Old-Smoke and your father Tekanondo favor this paleface's coming. They see no shame in befriending Englishmen."

"But I am not like my family," Young-Wolf insisted.

Captain looked through the scattered log cabins to the first blockhouse near the center of the town. "As long as you live in that English-built forthouse, I cannot be certain of any truth in your words."

"The house was abandoned by the English! They never even lived in it."

"If your father were still a strong warrior, I do not think he would have chosen this place to raise his sons."

Young-Wolf lowered his gaze.

"You know what meaning is carried by my words," Captain went on. "There was a time when your father could take fifty to sixty deer in one season. He supplied food not only for his family but for many others as well. But now disease makes him lame—as lame as the white man who hobbled into town. Consider, Ha-ga, it is *weakness* to depend on the English for supplies and ammunition. And it is a weakness that seems to stalk your family most of all."

"But I am strong! And I do not love the English. Give me another chance, and I will prove my loyalty to you."

"Look to your home, Ha-ga. Right now, Chief Old-Smoke and your father Tekanondo are leading that white man inside."

Young-Wolf's eyes would not lie. The man *was* at his door. "As long as Samuel-Kirkland shares my father's roof and my mother's fire, I will not be there," Young-Wolf pledged.

"And where will you be?" Captain asked.

Young-Wolf's neck tingled with sudden excitement. "I will be at the base of the Three-Oaks-That-Hold-Their-Heads-Together to look over Lake Ganundasaga. I will live as a warrior lives, with blankets and no fire. Then you see, Captain, that my words are rooted in my heart. Then you will know that you would be wise to think of me as one of your men."

Under Captain's steady eye, Young-Wolf strode home. He pushed open the blockhouse door and brushed past the white man who stood in the middle of the room, as though he were nothing more than a shadow on the floor. He gathered up a set of dry clothes and took down his father's traveling pouch from its peg on the wall.

"Where are you going?" Until that moment he had not seen his thin mother bending over the kettle on the hearth.

"To sleep in the forest," he announced. "I would rather share the night with the snow and ice than with this Samuel-Kirkland." The white man turned to look at him when Young-Wolf spoke his name.

Young-Wolf ignored his dark eyes. He went outside, passed his father and Captain in the dusk, and did not speak a word.

2

PALEFACE PROMISES

Young-Wolf watched from his cold cocoon in the bark lean-to as morning streaked the sky with pinks and grays. He stretched and rubbed his numb fingers. Deep within his blankets, under his thigh, lay the old stone knife that usually hung from his belt as a good-luck charm. He brought it out and pressed it to his cheek because it held what was left of his body's warmth.

Sliding out from his low bark shelter, Young-Wolf waded through the snow to the closest beech tree. He marred its smooth gray bark with his sharp-edged stone. Now there were ten rough marks lined up on the tree. Ten sunrises since the day Samuel-Kirkland had hobbled into town.

A chickadee tumbled through the branches and pulled Young-Wolf from his thoughts. "I wish I were you," Young-Wolf told him. "Every frozen moth and spider makes your stomach full."

He reached for the traveling pouch that hung against his right ribs. There was a pinch of parched

cornmeal for his breakfast in it. He grabbed the pow-
dered food with his fingers and ate it eagerly.

The chickadee watched and scolded him for his
greed. Young-Wolf shooed him away. "I've already
given my mother's soup and my own bed to a white
man," he complained. "I have no sympathy for lazy little
birds. Go find your own breakfast." In truth, Young-
Wolf liked Chickadee very much. Since his childhood,
Young-Wolf had come here often to learn the voices of the
forest. He and Chickadee had become friends during
those long, peaceful boyhood days.

Brother-Chickadee's drumming little "dee—dee—
dees" came back to Young-Wolf's ear. He tracked the
sound through the chilly air, and there, not more than
twenty paces from his camp, Samuel-Kirkland stood offering Chickadee crumbs from his own hand as he
munched on English bread!

Young-Wolf was angry. Angry at himself for not see-
ing the intruder. Angry at Chickadee who so easily
sought food from another source. He rushed toward the
bird and Samuel-Kirkland, clapping his hands. "Ha-ga!
Little-Brother! Be gone," he yelled. Chickadee flashed
off into the trees.

The paleface, however, stood firm though his hand
had shaken. His brown eyes looked at Young-Wolf
calmly. Young-Wolf squinted back. *Ahh, if I could speak
to you!* Young-Wolf's thoughts raged. *I would tell you to
get out of the forest. It is bad enough to have you in the town.*

Bold Chickadee came to them again. "Ha-ga!"
Young-Wolf shouted for a second time, but Samuel-
Kirkland, with kind eyes, pleaded for silence. Slowly the

paleface unfurled the hand of hospitality to Chickadee again. This time the bird came down onto Samuel-Kirkland's smallest finger and grabbed a bite of bread from his palm. The white man laughed as Chickadee flew off with his prize.

"Ot-kayason," Samuel-Kirkland whispered. He nodded to the bird in the tree.

Young-Wolf's eyes stretched wide. The man was learning to speak Seneca. "Ot-kayason. What is this?" he had said.

Young-Wolf shrugged, pretending not to understand.

The white man gave a nervous little smile and shrugged back. He nodded and walked away. Young-Wolf watched the spring in Samuel-Kirkland's step as he headed through the snow toward the lake. His legs had healed. Now even the forest might not be far enough away for Young-Wolf to avoid him. As he was thinking this, odd sounds rang through the trees. *"Ah thou my soool bless God the Looo-ord . . ."* The white man was singing as he walked. Young-Wolf abruptly turned his back on the noise.

A feathertip from behind one oak caught Young-Wolf's attention. The toe of a moccasin appeared beside another. Then Captain and three of his followers, including Bear-Lad, stepped into view.

Young-Wolf hid his surprise.

"So you are still camping under the Three-Oaks?" Captain said as he inspected Young-Wolf's lean-to with the hard instructor's eye.

"Yes," Young-Wolf answered proudly. "I have seen

ten sunrises from here. I have eaten only the meager food of a warrior, and for most nights, I have lived without a fire."

Captain smiled. "You are a very determined boy," he said. "And just how many days do you plan to stay away from Ganundasaga?"

"Until Samuel-Kirkland leaves," he said flatly. "I know white men. They take what they can from us. Then when their bellies are fat and satisfied, they move on."

Captain glanced at his men. Young-Wolf could see them sharing thoughts. "This white man plans to stay. Council has heard the message carried by the wampum belt from Johnson Hall. This Samuel-Kirkland comes as Sir William Johnson's friend. Chief Old-Smoke and Tekanondo have persuaded the leaders to let him live in Ganundasaga."

"To do what? He is not a trader or a hunter—he didn't even carry a gun."

"Truly. His being here is a greater threat. He comes saying that he wants to learn our language well, so he can someday speak to us from what he calls the Book of Hawenio."

"Book of Hawenio?" Young-Wolf looked at Bear-Lad. "Hawenio is the Great Power and the Great Good Voice. How could Father or Grandfather believe such paleface promises? Why would Hawenio choose a white man to bring us his word?"

Captain put a hand on Young-Wolf's shoulder. "Perhaps we stand closer than I knew. You see, I too wonder at these things."

Bear-Lad chewed his lip. "I worry for our young brothers, Young-Wolf," he said. "What if they are not wise enough to stand against this paleface's lies?"

Young-Wolf's eyes searched the treetops. "Here is a plan. Let's take all our cousins and brothers deep into the woods until this troublesome man is gone."

"Ahhh sing a new song to the Lord sing all the earth to God . . ." The breeze that carried the white man's English words teased the feathers in the warrior's hair. Captain and his men, straight-faced and sober, watched through a break in the trees as Samuel-Kirkland waded the snow back toward town.

When he finally disappeared, Bear-Lad whispered, "Who do you think he sings to?"

Young-Wolf eyed him sternly. "Don't even think about it—or you may find yourself growing weak as a chickadee while you search the meaning of the white man's trail."

Captain agreed. "Stay far from him, my Bear-Clan brother."

"We will!" Young-Wolf promised. "And we could start now to make a safe camp for all the younger boys."

Captain frowned. "No, Young-Wolf." He paused. "Today when the sun climbs to his highest point, Chief Old-Smoke will hold a special meeting in the council house . . . so that your grandmother and he can adopt Samuel-Kirkland *as their own son.*"

A stone slid into Young-Wolf's stomach. "What! Samuel-Kirkland, a brother to my father and Chief Old-Smoke's own child?"

Captain nodded. "We have come to tell you that

you must go home. The chief wants you at the ceremony. After today even *you* will have to call Samuel-Kirkland brother."

"You cannot let this happen!" Young-Wolf shouted. Captain's eyes narrowed. "Even adopted white men have been known to die in Seneca hands. We will watch. We will wait. And someday we will find a way either to kill Samuel-Kirkland or to drive him from our land. We are Senecas, and there is no need for white men in Ganundasaga."

"I want to be counted with you," Young-Wolf exclaimed. "I want you to know that even when the vile-tasting word of brother is on my lips in the council house, it will never reach down to my heart."

"Walk with me," Captain said as he led Young-Wolf ahead of the other men. "Perhaps I can use you, even though you're young." His voice was low as he surveyed Young-Wolf's face with burning eyes. "Stay alert. Be wise, for sometime when you least expect it, I will make you a partner in our plans."

Young-Wolf entered the dark, bark-sided council house. Chief Old-Smoke, big as a bear, greeted him. He wore a disk of shining silver at the hollow of his neck, a fine linen shirt, and rows of glass and wampum beads. "See where our family sits," he said, pointing to the cluster of Turtle and Wolf Clan people who were near the council fire. "Be with them, my son."

Young-Wolf walked to the front of the council house. He sat crosslegged on the floor beside his tall dark-skinned father. His mother at his other side smiled and touched his arm. He realized how much he had missed her soft round face and her gentle eyes. Two-year-old Baby-Brother was asleep in her lap. Suddenly Young-Wolf was hungry to be home. He wanted peaceful days and nights—*and no white brother.*

But Chief Old-Smoke had already led Samuel-Kirkland to the front of the narrow meeting hall. The white man sat down between the dark chief and a burly yellow-haired white man named Wemple-the-Blacksmith, who was paid by Sir William Johnson to be the town's interpreter and mender of their supplies. Across the fire from Young-Wolf's family sat the village leaders.

One of Grandmother's brothers, a respected clan leader, stood up and began to speak. "Open your ears. Open your eyes. See that we have a white-skin-brother in our midst. Since he has left his own mother and home to be with us, our sister desires to take him as her son. . . . From this day on he shall be called our White-Skin-Brother."

Young-Wolf curled his fingers into fists. *How could this be happening?* His ears stung with the last words of the formal adoption speech. ". . . now you of our nation be informed that this man has ceased forever to be called by his birth-nation's name, because it has been buried in the depths of the earth. Henceforth, let no one mention his original name or nation of his birth. To do so will hasten the end of our peace."

Looking down the row of leaders' faces, Young-Wolf's eyes met Captain's. The fire of anger he saw there heated his own heart.

White-Skin-Brother looked to Wemple. The two men exchanged quiet words. Then White-Skin rose with the chief. He spoke a strange rough mixture of English and Seneca, which babbled like a stream where two springs come together. Still Young-Wolf understood the things he said. "May God—Hawenio—the Great Good Voice—speak in his own way and show you that it is good for me to be called your brother. I thank Chief Old-Smoke, my father, and his wife, my mother, that I now have a Six-Nation family of my own."

He reached for Old-Smoke's outstretched hand. "Someday when I can speak our language well, my father, I promise to tell good stories of Hawenio for the kindnesses you show."

"Truly, my son," Chief Old-Smoke answered with smiling eyes, "already you are learning to speak well." His strong decorated body towered over the white man in his plain skin pants and linen shirt. "And now I want you to meet your family." One by one he presented Young-Wolf's relatives.

Finally the chief called Young-Wolf to his side. Young-Wolf looked at the dirt floor. "You may call him Ha-ga, which means *my younger brother*, for he is Te-kanondo's older son," Chief Old-Smoke said. "But among us, he is known as Young-Wolf, because he is a Wolf-clan mother's son."

White-Skin touched Young-Wolf's hand. "Greetings! Ha-ga!" he said with a smile.

Young-Wolf showed a wooden face, keeping his eyes dark. As soon as he filed past the man, he walked from the council-house door. Bear-Lad met him outside. "Well, what went on?" the boy asked.

"Why should you care?" Young-Wolf muttered. "He will never live under your roof."

Bear-Lad stepped in front of him. "And now he won't live under your roof either," he said with a grin. "He is part of Chief Old-Smoke's household now. He will stay right here in these living quarters at the end of the council house. So you can go home to your own bed. I am glad for you, even though you will have to call him brother."

"I will not call him brother." Young-Wolf smiled wearily. His time in the woods had made him hungry and tired. "You are a good friend, Bear-Lad, even if you did beat me out of a good knife. But your words do not raise my heart. I am angry at Samuel-Kirkland. I wish he had never come."

The other boy clucked his tongue as he put his hand on the knife in his belt. "Perhaps I will use this one day against your white man," Bear-Lad whispered. "You know, Captain watches for a reason to make Samuel-Kirkland die."

Young-Wolf swallowed hard. "But he is the chief's son," Young-Wolf reminded him painfully. "You understand our ways. To stab him would be to run a knife through Old-Smoke's own flesh and blood."

"Unless he does something to deserve punishment," Bear-Lad whispered. "Then, no matter what color his skin, he will face the tomahawk for that."

A young warrior with a missing right ear lobe came up to them. Young-Wolf knew that his English name, Isaac, in no way reflected a lack of Seneca loyalty. "Captain wants us in the forest at once," he said to Bear-Lad.

The boy nodded obediently. "We will talk again," he promised Young-Wolf. Then he went with Isaac, his lanky legs splitting wide like English scissors as he tried to keep pace with the tall sinewy man.

Young-Wolf sighed. He felt like White-Skin's little brother now—as alone and useless as a baby on his cradleboard.

But he walked away from Ganundasaga again because he remembered that his precious blankets and stone knife were still with the Three-Oaks near the shore. A half-moon rose over him in the orange afternoon sky, and still he stayed in his camp. Finally he tore down his lean-to and tossed its bark in all directions. Then he sat on his blankets tracing the chipped-off scallops on his knife's stone blade. Hungry wolves in his belly growled and tried to chase him home, but even they could not make him face his family's hearth fire. Thick darkness wrapped around him.

"Yoooung-Wolf . . ."

The low sound of his name made him jump against the black skins of night. He scurried to an oak and pressed his back against the bark. "Who's there?" his words trembled in the cold night air.

A human form floated toward him on the shadow-marked snow. The tree gnawed Young-Wolf's backbone, as the face came close enough for him to see the eyes, the large straight nose, the scar.

"Captain!"

"I desire your help."

Young-Wolf stepped from the tree. His hands chilled. "I am willing. What shall I do?"

Eerie moonlight danced in the warrior's eyes. "I have decided that you will be my spy. Because you are

Samuel-Kirkland's brother now, he will easily let you be his friend. Then you will be my eyes and ears. And everything you find out about him, you will report to me."

"Yes, I will do this," Young-Wolf pledged.

Captain's eyes became dark lines. "To succeed, you will have to convince your family that you want to be his loyal friend."

Young-Wolf tried to swallow. "This is a hard thing you ask of me, for I hate all who are not Indian." He paused, hoping for Captain's reply, but the warrior waited silently in the snow.

"I will do it—for you," Young-Wolf said at last.

"Fine," Captain's face showed a slit of a grin. "Now understand. This is our secret. No one can know that I spoke to you about this plan."

3

A Secret Splits the Heart

Young-Wolf lay on his bed, his belly burning with hunger but the rest of his body too comfortable to move. The smell of boiling corn bread sneaked around the deerhide curtain that separated his sleeping quarters from the rest of the house. He raised himself on his bunk to let the aroma tease his nose.

Even though his home was built by English hands, his father had put in two traditional Seneca sleeping chambers. These were made from poles and deerskin. They lined the wall facing the stone chimney and hearth. Each chamber was deep enough for a man to sleep lengthwise with his head to the outer wall and his feet toward the fire. Above and below the built-in beds there was space for storing wood, blankets, tools, and their few extra clothes.

Young-Wolf finally climbed from his bed. He dressed, pushed the skin curtain back, and joined his mother by the fire.

She pulled her iron kettle from the heat. "I thought the sun would walk across the whole sky before you left your bed." She looked at him with sweet, tired eyes, and Young-Wolf noticed how frail she seemed in her soft green overdress that hid all but a hem of a darker broadcloth skirt. It was white man material, but she had made it Seneca by decorating the neckline and sleeves with intricate beadwork.

Young-Wolf stretched his arms, soaking up the warmth from both the fireplace and his mother's gaze. He sat down on the narrow bench at the end of their rough split-log table. "I don't mind telling you that it feels good to be home," he said.

His mother nodded. "Even the warrior enjoys his fire when he comes in from the cold." She handed Young-Wolf a steaming hunk of bread on a smooth bark slab. Then in his own wooden bowl, she ladled out some of the liquid in which the white bread had been cooked. He ate the hot bread and drank the delicious beverage in sips from his carved wolf's-head-handle spoon.

His mother sat down across from him at the table. Baby-Brother, who had been toddling around the room with a corncob in his hand, climbed up to her. His chubby little hands combed through her long, loose hair. "You stayed away because of White-Skin-Brother, didn't you?" she asked, plopping Baby onto her lap.

Young-Wolf nodded. "I was waiting for him to leave Ganundasaga, but now he is my brother . . ." He paused, remembering Captain's urgent words. "So I've . . . I've decided to trust Grandmother's wisdom and give him a chance to be my friend."

A sparkle momentarily replaced the fatigue in Mother's eye. "This will please your father very much,

Young-Wolf. He has been concerned about your feelings toward White-Skin-Brother."

Again the memories of Captain's dark eyes haunted him. He pinched his hand. "Father has no reason to be worried now," he lied. "I will do what I can to make the white man welcome here."

His mother studied his face so long that he feared she could see the lake of untruth in his mind.

"You have made me wonderful food," he said abruptly, trying to shake her gaze.

"Young-Wolf," she said, rocking Baby against her chest, "I know you struggle with having White-Skin here. I understand. I was just like you when I was young. I was determined never to let the white man change my ways."

He looked around at her iron cookware, the woolen blankets, and the rifle hung on the rafter overhead.

"I know it's hard to believe," she insisted. "But I was like that. I bothered the grandmothers until they taught me how to make little old-fashioned clay pots for my cornhusk dolls. I saved the shoulder-blades of deer to make my own planting tools." Her memories seemed to brighten her cheeks.

"What happened?" Young-Wolf asked, taking the last spoonful from his bowl. "You are not that way now."

She showed a slight, girlish grin. "I came to love the son of the great Turtle-Clan Chief Old-Smoke," she said quietly. "And Old-Smoke reared his family to be friendly to Sir William Johnson and open to many English ways. So I—" A cough started deep within her. It shook her body and bowed her head before it stopped.

When she looked at Young-Wolf again, her gentle face seemed to have aged. Young-Wolf sighed. Without thinking, he went around the table and pulled his drowsy little brother from her lap. "Where is Father?" he asked tensely. "Does he know that this illness has come again?"

His mother trembled as the rattling cough shook her again. "He has gone to see if the she-bears are stirring yet from their winter dens. There is so little game anymore. But your father is convinced that this meat is what I need. The flesh of a strong animal will make me strong again, he says."

Baby-Brother stiffened in Young-Wolf's arms. His mouth twisted like that of one of the Faces, those trained healers with ugly wooden masks who danced and sang to cure diseases. "Perhaps there is some magic we have not yet tried," Young-Wolf suggested as his brother began to cry. "Somehow we must stop the evil that steals your breath away."

"No," she protested weakly. "We have tried everything. I think your father is right. I need meat and I need rest."

Young-Wolf kept his brother in his arms. "I'm taking Baby to Younger-Sister's house. Then you can rest and wait for Father. I want you to be well."

"When you worry, Young-Wolf, I see your father's handsome face on you." She picked up the bowl that he had wiped clean of food and stood to hang it back on the wall. Even this light work seemed too much for her.

"You rest!" he said as he wrapped Baby in a piece of soft doeskin. "I do not want this terrible cough back in our house."

Young-Wolf carried Baby outside. The day was clear and bright, but a sharp wind was blowing. Under his cover, Baby screamed as Young-Wolf raced along the snowy path to Mother's-Sister's bark house at the edge of town. He was just at her door when Isaac and Bear-Lad stepped in front of him. "Taking care of babies, too?" Isaac asked harshly. "You really are becoming a woman among Seneca men!"

"If I had a tomahawk, I'd crush your skull!" Young-Wolf snapped.

"It would be as likely that a fish would have wings," the warrior teased. "Captain will never think of putting a war weapon into your hands."

Young-Wolf bounced Baby angrily. Above the little boy's screams he confronted Bear-Lad. "What is the reason for these sudden evil words?" he asked. "You're my friend. You tell me."

Bear-Lad looked embarrassed. "Don't you know?" he said. "Captain has told us everything."

"Told you what?" Young-Wolf demanded.

"How Chief Old-Smoke convinced you to be Samuel-Kirkland's friend. And how you came to Captain in the night to say your mind is set now: You never want to be a part of Captain's men."

"And you believe this?" Young-Wolf raged.

Isaac's teeth clenched. "He is Captain! Say one word against him, and I'll cut out your tongue."

Bear-Lad's eyebrows knotted. "He warned us to stay away from you, Young-Wolf, until your senses return."

"I have my senses! Ask Captain!" Young-Wolf cried.

Suddenly Mother's-Sister was pulling on the fringes of Young-Wolf's shirt. She grabbed Baby. "Haga! Get in the house! What is going on?"

He looked to Bear-Lad for support, but the boy rested his hand on his knife pouch and walked away with Isaac.

In Mother's-Sister's dark home, Young-Wolf threw himself into one of the four sleeping compartments that lined the walls. Mother's-Sister came to sit at his feet as he hid in the darkness.

"Please tell me what is wrong," she said.

"Mother is sick again," he shouted. "Isn't that enough to make me feel this way?"

She touched his ankle. "It is enough. But that is not everything that troubles you." She unwrapped Baby and kissed him on his cheeks to dry his tears. "Come, my sweet little one," she cooed to him. "I will take care of you."

Young-Wolf watched her silently. In her youthful beauty there was a reflection of how Mother must have looked when her eyes had seen only fourteen summers.

"What is this I heard outside about you and Captain?" she asked after much silence.

Young-Wolf remembered Captain's ghostly form in the night. He realized now what a painful secret this was to bear. "There is nothing to say," he answered harshly as he pushed past her and put his feet to the floor. "But there is something I must *do*."

"Be careful," she pleaded. "Captain can be a cruel man."

"Don't treat me like a child." His words whipped back.

She nodded. "All right, my brother. Do what you must, and don't worry about your mother. I will spend the day with her—and more if necessary."

Outside the house he held his head high and listened to the air. He could hear voices taunting and teasing in the clear fields behind the large cluster of Wolf Clan homes. He walked to the sounds, and—as he had both hoped and feared—Captain was there with perhaps all of his twenty men.

The warriors were spread as far as the eye could see across the glaring snow. They had iced a straight, raised trough through the clearing. Now they were taking turns at gliding their long "snowsnake" sticks down the chute in the snow. Since they played for hides and rum, emotions were high. Shouts and hoots rang out as each contestant forced his snowsnake to fly through the snow. Captain stood watching the competition from the trees in the nearby chestnut grove. Young-Wolf gathered his courage and went to Captain.

"I desire to know why you set my brothers against me!" he said firmly to the warrior.

Captain slowly looked down at him. "I should not speak to such arrogance, Young-Wolf, but I will. Do you not remember your promise for even one day?"

"I promised loyalty and that I would not talk about your plans," Young-Wolf seethed. "But I did not promise that I would separate myself from those I call friend." He stood trembling with fear.

Captain pulled on the rows of beads and trinkets that lay against his chest. "When you decided to be a friend to Samuel-Kirkland, you decided *against* being friends with your Seneca brothers."

"But I am not White-Skin's friend!" Young-Wolf protested. "I am pretending this—just to please you."

"You promised to show this friendship to your family. That is your first task. I have convinced my men of your friendship with the white man. That was my first task."

A lump grew in Young-Wolf's throat. He took in a deep breath and raised his head. "I understand what has been done," he said miserably, "and I will not fail to do my part."

"I know why I favor you." Captain smiled. "There is courage in you that even the cold waters of the river could not show."

Young-Wolf could no longer look at Captain's face.

"It will take great bravery to stand against this man. There are powers at work in him that lie silent in other white men. Those who trust in guns can be destroyed with guns. Those who try to bribe with trinkets and supplies can be, and have been, bribed with Seneca promises of peace. But Samuel-Kirkland comes to bring us the white man's Book of God, and that is a threat to our beliefs. If he succeeds in making Indians believe white man's religion, then our people cannot call themselves Senecas anymore."

Captain raised his face to the sky. "White men come among us for land and game—but until Samuel-Kirkland walked to Ganundasaga, I never met a paleface who meant to steal the treasures hidden in an Indian's heart."

Just as Captain's words fell on the air, White-Skin came out to watch the snowsnake competition. The war

chief nodded toward the fields. "Go to him, Young-Wolf . . . and a warrior's courage be with you."

With heavy feet Young-Wolf approached the white man. He forced himself to touch his hand. "White-Skin-Brother," he said as cheerfully as he could. "This is called snowsnaking." He pointed to the men in the crowd. "Come. I will show you—*ga-wa-sa*—snowsnake."

White-Skin seemed both surprised and pleased with his sudden kindness. "I am grateful to you, Haga," he said in Seneca. "With you, I learn more." He followed Young-Wolf to the edge of the contest area.

Isaac pranced up to them, his body limber, his face glistening with sweat. "Tell me, the white man wants to play," he said with a grunt.

"I don't think so," Young-Wolf replied weakly. "I was just showing him what the game is like. He wants to know."

Isaac looked down his long nose. "And now that you are his friend you do as *he* wishes. Is this not true?"

Young-Wolf made himself ignore the remark. "I am only helping him to learn our language," he said coolly.

"Hah. Well, make sure he knows that it takes more than a skillful tongue to speak as a Seneca. Our bodies and our actions have languages of their own." Isaac shook his long scalp lock, jingling the coins that hung from the wire hoop in his ear. Mockingly he stretched his stick toward White-Skin. "You toss it," he teased.

White-Skin took it.

Young-Wolf held his breath as his white brother walked toward the end of the trough.

"What does he think he's going to do?" Isaac questioned angrily. "Throw my stick?"

Young-Wolf shrugged and trotted after his new companion.

White-Skin put his finger to the tip of the snowsnake. He took aim and let it fly. The stick whizzed cleanly down the trough and out of sight.

Isaac glared, "My snake has never been so slow!" he huffed.

"But look!" Young-Wolf challenged. "His throw was greater than that of the younger men. I can tell from here." Young-Wolf glanced at White-Skin in amazement. The white man's eyes were dancing.

"Tell him to go fetch my stick," Isaac ordered Young-Wolf.

"I don't speak his language," Young-Wolf reminded him.

But White-Skin pointed and nodded. "I go," he said in Seneca.

Isaac let White-Skin start across the field. Then he sprinted after him. When the white man saw the warrior behind him, he started running, too. They ran side by side until they reached the stick. White-Skin paused while Isaac retrieved his snowsnake, and then the two men raced each other back. Isaac's feet pounded home through the wet snow ahead of White-Skin's, but still the young white man had run fast enough to make most of the warriors gather around for another look at him.

While the men were still exchanging glances, Young-Wolf's father limped across the field to join them. White-Skin smiled when he saw him coming, and a look of approval was in the eyes of Young-Wolf's father, too. "My younger brother, you did well," he boasted. "In time these men may accept that you have been made a Seneca, too." He looked through Isaac's threatening stare and squeezed the muscle of White-Skin's upper arm. "By the time the strawberries bloom," he said with a chuckle, "you may outrun the deer."

White-Skin laughed. "Your words are very kind, or you have very slow deer in Ganundasaga. I do not know which it is—"

"Ho-hoo, you learn even to joke as an Indian," Young-Wolf's father cheered.

Young-Wolf looked around. Only his father was smiling. The rest of the warriors wore solemn faces.

His father, too, seemed mindful of the warriors' mood, but still he spoke to Young-Wolf. "I am grateful, Son, that you have shared the sunlight of friendship with our brother." Tekanondo's eyes walked from face to face so that every man knew the meaning of his words.

Young-Wolf's heart split into halves. *If Father knew I was no more a friend to Samuel-Kirkland than any of these other men, what would he do?* He felt the hateful stares of Captain's men. *Soon I will be forced to betray either Captain or my father. For no one survives rough waters by dividing himself between two canoes.*

His father nodded. "Come, Young-Wolf. Let's take our brother home. Your mother is well enough to be at Chief Old-Smoke's dwelling for the evening meal." He turned and started back toward town with White-Skin. Young-Wolf followed them, but from the corner of his eye, he could see Captain grinning under the chestnut trees.

4

CRIES IN
THE NIGHT

After their meal of dried squash stew and ash-baked bread, Young-Wolf and his father and grandfather stretched out on the cornhusk mats by the fire. It burned brightly under the framed-out smoke hole at the edge of the room. Grandmother had served the food while Mother rested, and as she took their empty bowls away, the men lit their pipes.

White-Skin lounged with them, as though he had been an Indian all his life. His darker-fleshed brothers laughed as he pieced together new words he had come to know. When they hooted, he repeated the phrase, taking better care at how his tongue performed.

"How did you learn snowsnaking?" Young-Wolf's father asked. "Your skill surprised everyone—whether they would show it or not."

White-Skin drew his knees up to his chin. "I do not think I have enough words to speak this big a story. It has much to do with my past."

"It is all right, my brother," Young-Wolf's father assured him. He tapped Young-Wolf's leg. "Run to get

Wemple-the-Blacksmith, Son," he said. "The man can translate for us."

Young-Wolf went into the cold, dark night. Moonlight drew a path to Wemple's cabin door. Young-Wolf knocked in the Englishman's way. In a moment Wemple came out sleepily, his tattered linen shirttail falling outside his breeches.

"Father wants you to translate White-Skin-Brother's words." Young-Wolf stood on his toes so he would not feel dwarfed by the powerful man.

"Samuel Kirkland's words?" Wemple chuckled. "Why the man already speaks Seneca about as well as I do, but if Tekanondo wants me, I'll be right there." He disappeared into the dark house to grab his own pipe and pouch, and soon they were back by Grandmother's fire. The room now was spicy with freshly brewed sassafras tea, and Young-Wolf found himself dipping his spoon again and again into the hot kettle as the men spoke.

"Find out how he learned snowsnaking," Grandfather said.

The blacksmith talked to White-Skin with sweeping movements of his huge stained hands. White-Skin softly answered him.

"He comes from a large family with very little English money," Wemple explained. "His father sent him to live with Doctor Eleazar Wheelock so he could be schooled."

"I know the man," Chief Old-Smoke said. "He taught the young Mohawk Joseph Brant English speaking and writing."

White-Skin nodded. "Yes. Joseph Brant was my

closest friend. There were six students at school—five of them Indian. And me."

"See, Tekanondo, he hardly needs an interpreter," Wemple laughed.

White-Skin grinned and talked to Wemple in English again. Soon the blacksmith translated his words.

"He was nineteen years old when he went to the Doctor's school. He is now twenty-four years old. Because he has had Indian friends, he has learned as much as he could about Indian ways, including games. But his desire to be among the native people of this great land goes back much more than this."

He paused while Chief Old-Smoke's wife laid two pieces of wood onto the fire.

"In Connecticut where his family lived, his heart was touched by the native people who had survived white man diseases and the takeover of land. From the time he was younger than Young-Wolf, Mister Kirkland has had a desire to raise the hearts of the Six-Nations people with good news from the Book of Hawenio."

The room was silent. "Now what else do you want to know?" Wemple looked from one to the other as he dipped in a spoon for tea.

"Ask him if he misses his family," Young-Wolf's mother said softly from the edge of one of the sleeping compartments across the room. Young-Wolf looked at her. It was good to see her relaxed and slightly better.

Wemple translated her words and White-Skin's answer. "He does. And he says that he asks his Heavenly Father—whom he calls Hawenio among you—to keep them safe."

"Does he have a wife?" Grandmother, in another sleeping compartment, put out her head to ask.

White-Skin's face grew pink as Wemple questioned him. While the yellow-haired man was laughing, White-Skin spoke for himself. "I am not married. If Hawenio so directs, someday I may be." He looked at his white companion. "Some answers are not safe to trust to an interpreter's tongue," he teased.

"If you can understand so well, why use an interpreter at all?" Young-Wolf was shocked that the question escaped his lips so easily.

White-Skin studied Young-Wolf's expression. "The leaders of the Six Nations know the answer to that very well. The beauty of a message comes not only from its meaning but also by the way it is spoken." He pointed to Chief Old-Smoke. "Your own grandfather is well-known among Indian and white leaders for his skill in weaving speeches out of words."

The chief nodded, thanking White-Skin for the compliment before his new son went on. "I know that Indian sons study under their Indian fathers to learn this precious art. That is why I give thanks for being here. It is my desire someday to be used as Hawenio's speaker for the people dwelling in this place. It is a path I see in my mind, Ha-ga, but I have only started down the trail a little way."

"You have walked farther than you think, my son." Chief Old-Smoke's eyes sparkled with respect. "From this day on, I say, speak without Wemple's help."

"Only if you keep scolding me when I use the wrong words, my father." White-Skin smiled. "I am grateful for your patience. Even now the stories of Hawenio swell within my heart. They beg my tongue to start my voice . . ."

"The oldest member in the group usually tells the fireside stories, my son, but you have my permission to speak."

White-Skin shook his head. "My words would fall like dead butterflies now. There would be no beauty in them at all. That is why I must wait. I must be as patient as an insect coming out from its caterpillar hut."

Chief Old-Smoke nodded. "When I received the wampum belt you carried from Sir William Johnson, I made a promise that I would protect you and provide for you and not ask you to tell stories from the Book of Hawenio until your tongue had learned our language well. I stand by that promise, my son."

"Well, this is beginning to sound very much like family talk." Wemple stretched out his bulging arms. "It's time for me to say good night." He stood and gave a hand to Young-Wolf's father, who was struggling to rise. "I see rheumatism is still plaguing your joints, Tekanondo," he said as he pulled the man to his feet.

Young-Wolf's father nodded silently. He limped over to help his wife out of the sleeping chamber. "Come, Young-Wolf. We must go to our house."

White-Skin-Brother followed them all outside. He started down the dark path between the council house and the Turtle Clan homes. "Where's he going?" Young-Wolf whispered. "I thought he was living here with Grandfather."

"He has been staying with your uncle instead," Father explained. "When Grandfather's warriors found out that the chief's new son has a clever tongue, they started coming into the council house day and night to talk with him. At my brother's house, White-Skin has time to rest and be alone."

Father's eyes tracked White-Skin in the moonlight until he neared the doorway of Uncle's neat hewn-log cabin. His watchfulness shook Young-Wolf. Father might already know something of Captain's dark plans, he decided. Even now, Young-Wolf's heart grew heavy with the part he had in them.

When they entered their own home, Young-Wolf relied on the weak glow from the hearth's coals to find his way to bed. He stripped off his breeches, pulled covers to his chin, and talked himself into sleep.

A moment later—or so it seemed—he awoke to horrid screams. "HA-WA-A-YOU! HA-WA-A-YOU! He is dead! He is dead!" Some poor woman in the village mourned.

Young-Wolf's father beat him out the door. They raced together along the path, as other men came running. The sobs rang from Uncle's own home, the one in which White-Skin stayed.

"I am Tekanondo—this man's relative!" Young-Wolf's father cried as he pushed everyone from Uncle's door. He burst inside, and Young-Wolf pressed in after him.

White-Skin was sitting at the edge of one sleeping compartment, with his head bowed down. Across from him, in the bed that faced the white man's own, Young-Wolf's uncle lay dead. Ugly shadows leaped onto the walls as Young-Wolf's father dipped a bundle of bark strips into Aunt's cooking fire to make a torch. He gave the blazing wood to Young-Wolf to hold so that Uncle's lifeless face could be made bright. Father knelt by his dead brother and sorrowfully ran his hands over the man's neck and chest.

"No marks," he said half to himself and half to Aunt, who stood watching him through her tears. "Tell me what happened."

"I don't know," she cried. "He was not sick."

Young-Wolf's father turned a dark face toward his white-skin-brother. White-Skin continued to hide his head in his hands.

The tossing light in Young-Wolf's hand trembled as men and women entered the small house to look upon the dead man's face and wail. Captain pushed his way through the crowd to Uncle's body. Bending over it, he put his fingers into the corpse's ears and nose and mouth.

"I have already looked for wounds," Young-Wolf's father told him. "There are none."

Captain responded with strange, half-closed eyes. "Some murderers do not need hands to bring on death," he answered solemnly. "There are spirits and powers beyond human ones that can carry out such evil."

Captain went to Aunt and turned her toward the light. Young-Wolf could see her face swollen with misery. "What magic did the white man work among you?" Captain whispered. "Tell me about any powders or sacred objects he carries, and let me know what spells and prayers have come from his lips."

The woman sighed into the palms of her hands. "White-Skin has been only gentle and kind. Sometimes he sings and prays, but it is often after the rest of us are in bed. He gets down on his knees to speak softly to Hawenio. That is all I know. He owns nothing more than an extra linen shirt, his writing sticks and, of course, the Book of Hawenio."

"The book!" Captain said triumphantly. "The evil power hides in there."

"My loved one's death has nothing to do with White-Skin-Brother," Aunt protested.

But Captain ignored her words. He walked to White-Skin's sleeping compartment, and while the paleface watched, Captain seized his pack from the shelf above his bed. He dumped the man's few possessions onto the floor. The Book of Hawenio tumbled out, spreading open before their eyes. Captain's face grew tense as he looked at the white paper with its small black marks. He picked up the book as one would a stinking carcass and carried it toward the fire.

"No!" White-Skin said in Seneca. "Don't burn the book!"

Young-Wolf's father lunged at Captain, grabbing the warrior's metal wristband. "You will not destroy my brother's paper words," he growled. "The council—not you—will decide what is to be done with him and with his possessions."

Captain snapped his arm free, and the book fell into Tekanondo's hand. In rage, Captain took the burning torch from Young-Wolf and brought it close enough to redden White-Skin's face. "You may not understand my words, Evil One, but you can understand my actions. When a Seneca dies, his death is avenged. And I will do everything in my power to see that you are tortured and killed to pay for the death of this Seneca man."

A shadow covered White-Skin as Chief Old-Smoke struck the torch out of Captain's hand. Young-Wolf's father kicked the smoldering bark back into the fire ring on the dirt floor. Then he stood beside his father.

Chief Old-Smoke seethed as his bulky chest and shoulders formed a stockade between Captain and his silent adopted son.

"You have no right to accuse my child of this death."

Captain's look sliced the chief like a knife. "I will not need to speak against *your son*," he retorted. "Tomorrow at council, the widow herself will call for Samuel-Kirkland's death. Then I and my men will see that he suffers long and hard for his crime."

Young-Wolf watched White-Skin's expression. His eyes were damp and quiet as a deer's before the animal gives itself into the hunter's hand. Though he hated White-Skin—and now feared his unseen powers, too— he hoped the man did not understand every word from Captain's tongue. It would be terrible to live through the night knowing that sunrise would bring torture and death at Captain's hand.

Chief Old-Smoke sat down beside his white son at the edge of the bed. He clutched White-Skin's wrists. "*Hawenio in every deed must do as he pleases.* Do you understand?" he said, staring into White-Skin's eyes.

White-Skin nodded.

"Then let these words comfort you, my son."

Captain paced in a tight circle around the fire, his long angry sighs sizzling like bear grease in the kettle.

For one brief moment when the warrior's back was turned, Young-Wolf's father pulled Young-Wolf into the pod of crying women. "You must hide White-Skin in Mother's sugarhut deep in the maple forest," his father whispered. "As soon as Captain turns his back again, grab White-Skin, go home for the rifle, and run like the wind."

"Me?" Young-Wolf gasped as the women's wails crawled in and out of his ears.

His father pushed White-Skin's book into his hand. "Go!" he said.

But suddenly the white man was speaking out loud. The din of mourning stopped as everyone listened to his strange sad words.

"He calls more evil spirits!" Young-Wolf breathed in terror. "Father, don't make me—"

His father threw a hand across his mouth. "He prays to Hawenio. Now get him and run."

With his eyes fixed on Captain, Young-Wolf worked his way across the crowded room. Slowly he reached for White-Skin's flesh. He caught the man's thin fingers, and at the right moment, he yanked him to his feet and dashed with him into the dawn.

"Run!" Young-Wolf coached as they raced between buildings. They burst through the blockhouse door, and Young-Wolf pulled White-Skin inside. Young-Wolf reached up on tiptoes to grab the rifle and shot pouch from the rafter. "Let's go," he said breathlessly.

But when he turned back to the open door, Bear-Lad stood watching. In shock Young-Wolf dropped the book. He ran to his friend, putting a free hand on his shoulder. "Don't tell Captain what I am doing," he begged. "It is Father who wants to protect White-Skin. Not me."

Bear-Lad wriggled free. "Get your fingers off me! They could be deadly as vipers now that *you've* touched the book." The boy dashed away into the shadows of the cabins.

Vines of fear twisted around Young-Wolf. "Come on!" he said to White-Skin, his hand sweating against the rifle barrel. The white man bent down for the Book of Hawenio, but Young-Wolf violently yanked him away. "There's no time for that! Come on!"

"Where are we going?" White-Skin asked as they stepped outside.

Young-Wolf refused to answer. Already the fields beyond the village rang with cries of "Gooh-weh! Gooh-weh! Gooh-weh!" as runners left Ganundasaga to announce Uncle's death to the surrounding towns. Young-Wolf looked toward the council house. The morning air vibrated with activity as women laid extra cooking fires for the funeral feast and Captain's men stockpiled barrels of liquor for the all-night drinking party that would follow.

White-Skin moved away. "I must go to the council house," he said. "Isn't it your custom to gather there to mourn a village leader's death? Your uncle was well respected. I must go to show my sorrow."

"You don't understand!" Young-Wolf raged, pulling him back. "If Aunt speaks against you in council today, Captain and his men will kill you!"

White-Skin nodded. "I do understand. I heard Captain's words. But truly, I am sad. I must say that to Aunt, her little girl, and others."

What am I to do now that White-Skin refuses to go with me? Young-Wolf fumed. His angry stare seemed to keep the man from moving. Then to his relief, he saw Father coming toward them.

"Good. You two are going to hunt squirrels," Father called out. "Because of those who will come for the condoling ceremony, I welcome the possibility of more food." Father's words were loud enough to attract the attention of two of Captain's men who rolled a rum keg along the path.

Father waited until the warriors passed. His arm fell across Young-Wolf's shoulder. "Captain's birds have ears," his father whispered. "And none of them must hear this. The chief and I have pledged White-Skin's safety to Sir William Johnson, and we must not fail to keep our promise."

Young-Wolf trembled. "Father, perhaps I am not the one to go with him."

His father squeezed his shoulder. "The chief or I would be missed at the condolence council, but you will not. Go and do not return until I send word to you."

Young-Wolf's stomach knotted up like a wounded lizard. He slid the rifle sling so that the gun and pouch of lead hugged his back.

Father turned to White-Skin. "Go with my son," he said. "I have made a pledge to keep you safe."

White-Skin nodded with a last longing look toward town.

"Don't leave footprints that can be followed," Father advised quietly. "Then I believe you will be safe."

Having no choice but to believe the wisdom of Father's plan, Young-Wolf led White-Skin out of Ganundasaga as his enemies looked on.

5

THE HIDEOUT

By afternoon the warm sun had turned the ankle-deep snow into cornmeal mush. Young-Wolf thought about Father's words as he looked back at the two sets of clear, wet tracks. He must cover their path or risk having bloodthirsty, drunken warriors follow them into the night. He motioned for White-Skin to stop. They waited on a fallen log until the sun was nearly down. Then Young-Wolf stood and dropped the butt of the gun against his toe.

He loaded the rifle, tamping a measure of powder, a spit-soaked cloth patch, and a lead ball to the bottom of its barrel with his smooth ashwood rod. Having poured powder into the tiny flashpan above the trigger, he clicked the frizzen down. Finally he checked the flint that would strike the metal and spark the powder. All looked ready. He squeezed the trigger and wasted the precious ball on the air.

"Why shoot at nothing?" White-Skin asked.

Young-Wolf hung the gun back on his shoulder and started retracing their steps. "The shot will make any of

Captain's men who listen think we are hunting here toward the Cayuga towns. Now we hide in the opposite direction, but we must hurry while we still have light."

"You are smart, Young-Wolf."

"There is no time for talking. One mistake and Captain will be on our trail."

They jogged toward the setting sun until they met a gurgling creek crisscrossed with fallen trees. Without a word Young-Wolf took off his moccasins and his leggings to keep them dry. He rolled them under his arm and waded into the cold water with bare feet.

Looking over his shoulder he saw White-Skin take off his moccasins and breeches to come in after him. The hem of the man's linen shirt hung out beneath his deerskin jacket and came down halfway to his knees.

They headed upstream over the logs. The icy water rose to their thighs before they came to the thickets of rhododendron that walled in both sides of the creek. Here Young-Wolf left the streambank and forced his way through the dark, leathery evergreens. Their woody stems whipped his freezing legs, but Young-Wolf did not stop to put on his clothes until his skin had dried. White-Skin followed his example.

By now the sun had gathered his light into the black pouch of night. White-Skin put his fingers against Young-Wolf's back so he would not be lost along the way. From the direction of the breeze and the feel of the ground beneath his feet, Young-Wolf chose their path. Eventually his hand came against the sugarhut door.

"I am amazed and grateful for your skill," White-Skin sighed as they shuffled into the deathlike cold of the long-closed cabin. Young-Wolf shut the door, though there was no bar with which to lock it. White-Skin's weary breaths echoed from the walls. Their legs scraped against the low shelves built on each side of the room. Young-Wolf's ears told him when his white brother came to rest along the wall opposite his own long seat.

Young-Wolf sat down and pulled his legs up under him. His thoughts were like tangled snakes waking each other in their winter dens. He was here to protect White-Skin from Captain—but who was here to protect him from White-Skin's magic? He reached for the stone knife on his belt. It was gone!

"Ha-ga?"

Young-Wolf refused to respond.

"Ha-ga," White-Skin said again. "You risk your life for me. I think Hawenio is pleased by this."

Suddenly the darkness filled with awful visions— dead Uncle's face . . . Aunt's tears . . . Bear-Lad's terror at Young-Wolf's touch. He quaked and laid his gun across his knees, feeling for the flint and trigger. In a moment it could be readied for firing. But as Captain had warned, it was a useless weapon against unseen powers and his darkest fears.

White-Skin started chanting to the night.

"Quiet!" Young-Wolf seethed. "Your enemies will find us." Inside he shook for a different reason. What spirit was White-Skin's voice meant to please? Suddenly Young-Wolf's teeth were chattering.

"What's wrong?" White-Skin asked. "I cannot see you, but I hear you trembling."

Young-Wolf wrapped his arms around himself. He wondered if White-Skin's power would harm him because he had made a promise to be Captain's spy. "We should be silent," he said, stepping around his terror. "Yes, I suppose," White-Skin answered him. "But if I am to die tomorrow, I wish to sing and pray tonight." "Father does not want you dead. That is why I bring you here." As Young-Wolf spoke, the thought of White-Skin's being burned or tomahawked caused his stomach to roll.

"I am grateful for your help, young friend."

"Don't call me *friend*." Young-Wolf moaned. "You are the chief's adopted son, but your tongue still is white. It knows nothing of the meaning of that word."

"Then teach me," White-Skin said. "That is why I came to Ganundasaga. Tell me what it means in Seneca to be called friend."

Young-Wolf put his head against the cold wall. He thought of Bear-Lad befriending Isaac now. The idea squeezed his tense and angry heart. "Friend means you protect each other. Friend means you will die for each other. A Seneca cannot choose his father, his mother, his brothers. But he can choose his friends."

"You are with me in this danger. Does this not mean you are my friend?"

"I do this for my father. . . . I will not say more."

"I am sorry that you have to be here with me. It's cold and dark, and you do not know me very well. But I am glad for your company."

Young-Wolf bit his tongue.

White-Skin whispered his chant again, but this time he sang Seneca words: "Father of peace and God of love, we own your power to save, that power by which our Savior rose victorious over the grave. . . ."

Young-Wolf listened. His whole body seemed to

freeze when the room grew silent. "Is this your death song, White-Skin?" he asked timidly.

"Death song? I do not know the meaning of these words."

Wishing he could see White-Skin's expression, Young-Wolf straightened. "A warrior sings his death song in the face of his enemy to prove that he is not afraid to die."

"Well, then, perhaps this is my death song." White-Skin sighed. "I know my enemy, but I sing praises to my God even as this foe stalks me to my grave."

Young-Wolf frowned. "I did not know a white man could speak so bravely. Still I am learning that strong words are useless without strong actions. When you meet Captain's hand tomorrow, then I shall see how brave you really are."

"Ha-ga, my enemy is not Captain. My enemy is the Evil One himself. This very night, using fear, he tries to make me leave my Savior's side. But I sing, because this Friend is stronger than even death itself. If Captain kills me tomorrow, my life will still go on in peace beside my Friend, Jesus Christ."

Young-Wolf drew his legs close to his chest. "I see no such friend. Where is he, and how can he follow you in both life and death?"

"He is the Son of Hawenio himself, who oversees life and death. He is the First Born of Creation, the Prince of Peace, the Beginning and End, the Living Water of Life . . ."

"These words are in your book?"

"Yes, Ha-ga, yes, they are."

Young-Wolf quivered at the excitement in White-Skin's voice. "Then I wish to hear none of it!"

"Why?"

Young-Wolf rolled himself to the wall, longing for the safety of his lean-to camp. "It is a white man's book."

"No—it was written long ago before Englishmen. It's the story of Hawenio and his dealings with all women and men. Hawenio himself has said that the things in this book must be told throughout the whole earth, and then he will show himself to mankind again. That is why I come to learn to speak your language."

"My ears are closed." Young-Wolf's voice rose. "I will listen no more." He held his arms to keep them from shaking. "For all I know, these same words may have led my uncle down the pathway of death." Young-Wolf stared at the darkness waiting for White-Skin's next reply. But soon all he heard was the slow, heavy breathing of the white man's sleep.

Toward dawn on their third day in the sugarhut, Young-Wolf saw a light flicker through the door cracks. Noiselessly he slid from his seat. By touch, he found a tiny swatch of cloth in the patch box built into the butt of his gun. He dropped the musty material onto his tongue, his heart drumming wildly. Silently he drew out the ramrod and pushed the powder, patch, and ball deep into the barrel. Then he lifted the rifle, filled the flash-pan, and stood ready to fire.

The door creaked. "Young-Wolf . . ." The voice was high and weak.

"Mother's-Sister!" Young-Wolf gasped as he slid

against the wall. "I almost shot you between the eyes."

"I'm glad you waited a moment to see who I was." The small light she carried showed her smile and lack of fear.

"You should not be here," Young-Wolf scolded.

"All is peace now," she announced. "Your father sent me. White-Skin can come home." She looked around. "Where is he? Is he all right?"

"Better than I," Young-Wolf complained. "He sleeps at night. I do not."

She laughed. "That's because there's a warrior inside you." She put down the glowing coals inside the nail-pricked tin, the light by which she traveled. "I have brought you some food," she said, slipping her basket straps from her shoulders. "I thought after two days you would be very hungry." The aroma of corn moved Young-Wolf to take a seat on the floor beside the basket of treasures. He did not tell her that he had risked the sound of rifle blasts and the evidence of a small fire to cook two black squirrels yesterday.

"It is weak soup. This is about all Chief Old-Smoke and his family have. The huge funeral feast used up almost all the food in Ganundasaga."

This was unhappy news. The time of starving would stretch through the next two moons.

White-Skin rose stiffly from his sleep and joined them next to Sister's basket. He smiled at the girl, and she smiled back as she filled two bowls. Her eyes warmed White-Skin's face. "Do you understand that you are free?"

"Don't be fooled," Young-Wolf said, feeling edgy.

"He understands words much better than you think."

"That is good," she said. "Then he will soon speak to us from his book."

White-Skin dipped his spoon. "Please tell me what has happened to the book."

Sister grinned. "Tekanondo keeps it safe for you. When you return, you will have it in the blockhouse loft where you will stay. From there he can keep a protective eye on you."

Young-Wolf did not hide his sigh.

"Truly, I have a great family . . . and a fine sister, who brings me food." The white man struck the ground with his right fist and raised his hand. "Thanks to you, Hawenio!"

Sister's eyes widened a bit. "It is well. You even pray in the style of our people now."

White-Skin smiled. "The Great Good Voice can use one's enemies to teach good things. The warrior Isaac on the snowfield told Young-Wolf that my body must learn to speak Seneca—so I copy how my faithful brother Te-kanondo gives his thanks to God."

A lump of anger swelled in Young-Wolf's throat as he watched how Sister hung on White-Skin's every word. "It is time to start the journey home," he said.

"There are two things I must tell," Sister replied as she packed her basket. "It was, of course, Aunt's words at the all-night council that saved White-Skin's life. She will speak only good of him, and now almost everyone in Ganundasaga believes her words are true."

"Captain, too?" Young-Wolf's mouth dropped open.

"No, he will not bury the axe, though the village council wants him to speak peace. This, too, you must know. He blames White-Skin for the funeral that hastens the season of starving, and he spreads stories of fear about how our departed one haunts Ganundasaga waiting for White-Skin to be put into a grave."

White-Skin closed his eyes. "I must work harder. Only the words of Hawenio can put out such evil wildfires."

"We should go," Young-Wolf said impatiently, getting to his feet. The others followed him outside.

"Captain and his men are like rattlesnakes in the town," Sister whispered to Young-Wolf. "They lie quiet now, waiting to use the venom that hides within their mouths."

"Why tell me?" Young-Wolf shrugged, pushing his rifle strap onto his shoulder.

Sister waited until White-Skin was far behind them. "Because you don't know which side to be on," she said softly. "I can see it in your eyes."

He walked in silence for a while. "Look," he said, brushing away Sister's words. "There are fresh claw marks on this maple trunk. If I can find the tracks of the bear who made these, it will be the path to many meals."

She shook her head. "So be it. I can lead White-Skin back to town alone. But, Ha-ga, be careful . . . and think about the news I bring you."

As soon as they disappeared, Young-Wolf breathed easier. It was good to be alone. He headed for the stream, swampy ground sucking at his moccasins. The bitter smell of skunk-weed stung the air. Where the first spring leaves of this plant unfurled, he saw fresh bear tracks in the muddy snow.

Jumping the creek where Bear had crossed, he followed the paw prints throughout the day. Finally, in a laurel thicket straight ahead, some movement caught Young-Wolf's eye. He watched, thinking of his gun. But alone, with even the most powerful charge, he probably could not take Brother Bear. It would be wiser to get Father and build a deadfall trap. That would lure the animal to bait and suddenly crush his skull with an avalanche of logs released by the triggering stick.

As Young-Wolf dropped low on bent knees in the sticky snow to observe his prey, he realized that buckskin—not bear skin—moved among the shiny evergreen leaves. Now that he knew he was sneaking toward a man, he grew even more alert. Closing in with skillful silence, Young-Wolf recognized the figure. He felt a surge of pride, having stalked him so well.

"Father!" Young-Wolf said, jumping out toward the skin-clad warrior who sat beside a stack of logs. "You're building a bear trap right here!"

"Young-Wolf!" his father laughed. "How did you find me?"

"I was tracking the bear that will fill this trap."

"Some bear I am." Father sighed as he rested from his work. "An old bear. A stiff bear—perhaps."

His words would have made Young-Wolf smile if they had not been so close to truth. His father's outstretched legs were like unbending oak.

"This is the right place for the trap," Young-Wolf said, trying to change Father's expression of pain. "Now that I'm here, I will help you build and set it."

"First, tell me about White-Skin-Brother. Why is he not with you?"

Young-Wolf shrugged nervously. "He has followed Mother's-Sister home. I thought that would be safe because of the council's decision."

Father frowned. "It will never be safe for him while Captain lives here."

Young-Wolf picked up Father's axe. "I am tired of thinking about this white man! I have carried the weight of his worries long enough."

His father struggled to his feet and clamped a hand on his shoulder. "I am grateful for what you have done for him."

"I will cut the saplings we need," Young-Wolf volunteered, anxious to free himself of even Father's company. He walked a short distance, slipped the gun and pouch over his head, and leaned his supplies against a wide beech tree.

Long fingers suddenly reached out and grabbed his arm.

"Captain!" Young-Wolf breathed. "What are you doing here?"

Captain pulled him behind the trunk. "You track bear. I track you," Captain whispered. "Now tell me what you've learned from two days with Samuel-Kirkland. Speak quickly, and your father will not have to know I am here."

Young-Wolf quivered. "Nothing . . . really."

Captain squeezed his wrist. "Tell me!"

"There is nothing," Young-Wolf said again. "He sings a lot. He talks a lot in our language now. That is all I know."

Captain frowned. "That is not much for having spent *two days* with him."

Young-Wolf hung his head. "I went hunting without him. I found I did not like being around him."

Captain jerked his arm. "I expect you to be my ears and my eyes. I want to hear something from your lips that will allow me to make him die. He is no less dangerous than smallpox or—"

Suddenly Father stood beside him. "Why is your hand on my son, Captain?"

"I speak to him of the foolishness of building a bear trap in the spring." Captain tossed his head. "This is not the season for hunting, Tekanondo, but perhaps you grow so white that you forget things like that."

Young-Wolf's father raised his chin. "My family is starving," he said without apology. "It is possible that Bear will see fit to give his life for us."

Haah!" Captain laughed. "You befriend White-Skin, so remember my words: *No bear will ever be in this trap*. You side with the destroyers of the land. Now you yourself will be destroyed." He pointed a bony finger. "Tekanondo, are your eyes sealed shut? Look at you— your brother dies, your wife is sick, your knees won't straighten anymore. The spirits sent by the Evil One have you. Give over the white man, and good spirits will befriend you again."

Young-Wolf's father walked away.

Captain called after him. "A stone thrown into the water does not make just one circle, Tekanondo. It makes many, many rings. Get away from Samuel-Kirkland, or like your brother, your life will be cut off."

Then Captain confronted Young-Wolf. "If you follow Tekanondo, you are on a dark path, too, and there will be no reason for us to speak again." The warrior stared at him a moment. Finally he raced away, the feathers in his hair flowing in the wind.

Young-Wolf came to Father. "Is there anything you wish to say to me?" his father asked.

Young-Wolf shook his head.

"Let us set this trap another day," Father said, crumbling the bait, a precious piece of tree sugar, into the breeze. "We give you this gift, Bear," he called out. "Now we ask that you give yourself to us in our desperate time of need."

6

THE STARVING TIME

Time walked slowly from the season of sugar-tree sap through the mud-filled days of early spring. It was a moon of waiting for the Senecas, a patient waiting for the trails to dry and a painful waiting for the first green plants that would ease their hunger and keep more of them from falling into that sleep of sleeps—starvation.

Young-Wolf cared little about where or how White-Skin waited out his time of famine. He had work to do: snowshoes to make, fields to clear, new graves to dig. There was little strength for even the simplest of his tasks and none to waste on things such as checking the ever-empty bear trap that had been built with Father's dreams.

When the buds of the bloodroot appeared like tiny white-haired Forest-People in curled green robes, Wemple-the-Blacksmith returned from his trips to Fort Niagara and Onondaga. As usual he had found reason to be away during the harshest days of hunger.

Because of the white man's report of food in some of

the Cayuga towns, Chief Old-Smoke sent some of his warriors with presents to trade for corn. When they returned, the small amount they had obtained was divided into even smaller portions and spread among the hungry in the town. Still the scant share of corn that Young-Wolf carried home encouraged Mother's heart. She prepared a meal of soup and bread, the first she had made in many weeks.

Father sat down to it with a happy face. He held Baby on his lap and shared freshly boiled bread with his ravenous little boy. "Climb the ladder, Young-Wolf. I am concerned because White-Skin is ill with hunger. He must share in this special meal."

Young-Wolf stared at his spoon.

"I want you to go," his father said again. "Perhaps you do not understand. Our White-Skin-Brother has been keeping himself from this table for just one reason—because he does not want to take from our precious food. If my legs would let me, I would go to him. But I cannot climb the ladder—this is why I ask you."

Anger slipped from Young-Wolf's tongue. "Use your voice. Call him down from there."

"No," Father said. "You do not know how weak he is. This morning I watched him crawl up to his bed. It is possible that you will have to take the food to him."

Young-Wolf put more spoonfuls into his mouth. When he could not delay his duty longer, he pulled himself away from the delicious meal and went to the loft.

Rain started plopping against the cedar shingles as he reached the top ladder rung. A dark gray square of sky showed through the window of the dim loft. White-

Skin was at his table, with his eyes closed and his head laid against the open Book of Hawenio. Young-Wolf had not seen him for many days.

The fingernails of hunger had dug deep wells between the bones of White-Skin's cheek and jaw. Young-Wolf grimaced at the sight of it. Then he tiptoed back to the ladder, glad that he would not have to talk to the man because he was asleep.

But as Young-Wolf stepped down, White-Skin stirred. He raised his head, and Young-Wolf saw his eyes red with silent tears. Young-Wolf waited, not knowing what to say or do. He hated the weakness that dimmed White-Skin's expression. By being there, he feared that the hand of death might take him, too.

"I am sorry . . . that you found me this way," White-Skin breathed. "I just can't seem . . . to fight this hunger anymore. My thoughts are all wrapped round my belly . . . I feel that I must eat . . . or I will die."

"You are sick, White-Skin," Young-Wolf said. "And Father is very concerned for you. That is why he wants you to come and eat."

"No . . . I promised him that I would earn some of my own bread during the starving time." He held the weight of his head in his hands. "But it is almost impossible to do."

"That is a promise you made to him. He did not ask it from you."

"I know." White-Skin sighed. "I know. But your family is starving, too. I cannot eat food that your mother and Baby so desperately need."

Young-Wolf looked away. "Mother has received corn for a special meal. It is food that Wemple located while on his travels and it was brought back by my grandfather's men. It is just one meal, but it is a gift to you from my father's heart."

"Truly, I am grateful. But I am troubled, too." White-Skin paused. "Tomorrow the kettle will be empty, but your bodies will hold on to the strength you dip from it today. My stomach, however, will have me starving again."

Young-Wolf avoided his dull eyes. "It does not surprise me," he said quietly. "The need for daily food is as white as your white skin."

White-Skin held up a thin hand. "Hawenio himself chooses how to make us. For this reason I would not ask him to change the color of my skin. . . . But I have been praying that he will change the color of my belly."

He gave a tired laugh. "I want to learn to live as you and your people do, Ha-ga. There is much wisdom in the way you fit your living to the land. I admire you greatly, for I have found that life as an Indian is very, very hard. Perhaps I should have gone with Wemple . . ." White-Skin rested his folded arms on the table. "He warned me that I would be a fool to try waiting out these moons of hunger."

Young-Wolf looked at him. "You could have gone with Wemple, yet you chose to stay?"

White-Skin nodded, swallowing with great difficulty.

"Why?"

"I thought . . . I thought I should show the people of Ganundasaga that I am willing to suffer with them. I have a family here. I have come to love them, and in hard times I should not walk away."

"But you are so weak, White-Skin. Here in Ganundasaga, what good can your weakness do?"

White-Skin turned his head away. "I am grateful for your honesty. I want to answer your question, but I would have to choose words from the book. I remember our talk in the sugarhut. Your approval would be needed before I could speak such words."

Nearing the table, Young-Wolf eyed the open pages. "I will listen with my ears," he decided, "while I put a guarding hand over my heart. If the words are good, I will let them go inside me. If they are not, I will shake them from my head and put them back into your book."

White-Skin's eyes gathered strength for a smile. "Truly, you are Chief Old-Smoke's grandson. The words you weave are no less beautiful than his. I pray you will like the Book of Hawenio, for it has beautiful pictures made with words."

Turning papers as thin as new beech leaves, White-Skin's hands came to rest beside the words that White-Skin changed from English into Seneca: "We carry the treasure of Hawenio's own spirit in our weak earthen vessels so that all who can see us can know that the power within us comes from Hawenio and not from ourselves."

He let out another weary breath. "I take my courage from those words. What do you think?"

"I am not ready to shake my head. And I am not ready to uncover my heart. But my mind will think on them, and later I will decide."

"Truly," White-Skin nodded, "every man must decide for himself what to do when he hears a word from Hawenio. Perhaps as we eat together you will think about the truth again. The contents of a kettle are much more important than the beauty or the strength of the pot."

Young-Wolf waited for the man to catch his breath. When he stood, he steadied himself against the table. Young-Wolf had to put an arm around his waist to help him out of the loft. White-Skin's ribs rubbing against his own felt like those of a wounded dying deer.

As soon as they reached the bottom rung, Young-Wolf's father helped White-Skin to the table. "My brother. Death pounds on your door."

White-Skin painfully lowered himself to the bench. "I am proof that the white man is not so good as the Indian when it comes to living on little food."

Mother dipped only a small amount of soup into White-Skin's bowl. "I am sorry, my brother," she said with tears in her eyes. "But if you put more than this in your stomach now, your stomach will toss it back at you."

White-Skin managed a smile. "I am grateful for your food and the wisdom on how to eat it." Then greedily he cleaned his bowl.

Father and White-Skin shared the last pieces of bread. "We must get you back to your people," Father said. "Otherwise you will go to your grave before the oak leaves grow to the size of a squirrel's hind paw."

"At least, if I go to the grave, I will not stay there." White-Skin's eyes brightened some. "We have talked enough that you know I believe Jesus Christ will meet me in death and lead me to Hawenio's side."

Father shook his head. "I cannot see your Jesus on the path to Hawenio. You may find comfort in that

name, but I do not. Those who murder us, take our land, and laugh when they can make us drunk with wine also sing your prayer songs and read from your Book of Hawenio."

Tears came to White-Skin's eyes. "That is why I am here. . . . That is why I pray that God—yes, Hawenio—will strengthen me so that I can stay. These people you talk about drag my precious Savior through the mud of shame. If it had not been for such men, I know you would have easily believed that Jesus Christ is Hawenio's own Son. . . . Tekanondo, your heart, like mine, knows that it must turn itself toward God."

Mother put another small spoonful of soup into White-Skin's bowl. "Eat a little more. Brother, you must not die."

White-Skin weakly struck the bench with his right fist. "I give thanks."

"It is well," Young-Wolf's parents said in unison.

Mother went to her bed to rest. "When you are stronger, I would like to learn how to look death in the eye as you do. It would be a gift to have peace instead of fear. Even warriors in Ganundasaga would welcome such a present."

White-Skin propped his head with his wrist. "I will tell you . . . when I can."

Father looked to Young-Wolf. "I think you should help him to the loft."

Young-Wolf shook his head. "He is too weak. He may have my bed."

White-Skin had grateful eyes as Young-Wolf supported him to his own sleeping quarters.

Father opened the door to let the gray light of the

day come inside. "If we only had the strength for it," he said looking at the rain, "I could get White-Skin home."

"Do not worry about it," White-Skin spoke from the sleeping chamber as he stretched out across the bed.

But Father continued to think out loud. "Six days' travel by canoe, and I could get you to an English fort. Less than a moon of travel, and I could take you the whole way to Johnson Hall. With a little more food to strengthen us, we could do these things."

7

STRENGTH FOR THE JOURNEY

While White-Skin and the family rested that afternoon, Young-Wolf sat by the fire. Suddenly Bear-Lad ran through the open door. He was dripping with rain. "I know I am not supposed to be here," he panted quickly, "but you have not noticed *in three days' time* that your trap killed a bear." The other boy disappeared almost before the words hit Young-Wolf's ears.

"A bear! A bear!" Young-Wolf hooted with delight. "A bear! A bear!" His heart was bursting with joy, until he saw Father's silent eyes.

"Three days, my son," his father said. "I thought you were checking the trap."

"I was. For days." Young-Wolf hung his head. "Then I lost hope. I . . . I began to believe Captain's curse on it. I . . . I'm sorry, Father."

"Sorry?" Father said. "Your carelessness might have stripped the last hope for life from this family." He limped to his sleeping chamber and took his long hunting knife from the shelf. "Come. We must save what we can of the meat and hide. Hopefully, all has not been lost in the heat of three days."

The rain beat down on Young-Wolf as he walked behind his father. When they approached the trap, his nose told him they would look at rotting meat. Without hesitation Father slit the she-bear's belly and dug out the swollen, stinking entrails. Young-Wolf sucked in breath and joined him. His throat strained to hold down his last meal. Rain and blood mixed together as they worked to strip the hide.

By evening they had rescued the fur and some of the hindquarter, the only part that wasn't riddled by the work of bugs and flies. The rain stopped, but still they were soaked to the skin. On the way home they stopped at the creek to wash the meat and their own vile-smelling bodies. The flesh they brought back went into Mother's largest pot. Soon the house reeked of rancid bear grease, but when the stew was ready, White-Skin got up from Young-Wolf's bed to join them for a second meal.

Young-Wolf lifted the hot gray liquid toward his mouth. Then he saw some of the meat move. He dropped his spoon, hoping Mother wouldn't notice. Fat worms stirred the broth with their wriggling! He glanced at White-Skin's bowl. His soup was moving, too. White-Skin looked at him, and Mother caught their eyes.

Her own filled with tears. "This is bad soup, very bad soup."

"No! No!" Father said, slurping down three spoonfuls. "I am grateful. You made it very well."

Young-Wolf watched his father's brother. The man closed his eyes and put the twitching broth into his

mouth. He swallowed, filled his spoon, and did it again.
Mother handed White-Skin a small basket of salt.
"Here," she said. "We do not eat salt as the white man
does, but perhaps it will improve your meal."

White-Skin nodded. He tossed in a big pinch of the
white powder. Then he ate every bite—wiggling or still—
that was in his bowl. His eyes welled with tears, and
Young-Wolf could not tell whether he laughed or cried.

"A meal of spring bear meat does make one feel
very much *alive*," White-Skin said as he got up and hurried out of the house with his hand over his mouth.

"And a full rack of bear meat could have *kept* us all
alive," Father said, his eyes burning with anger.

Young-Wolf pushed himself from the table, walked
to his sleeping chamber, and threw himself down on his
bed behind the deerskin curtain. In a short while, he
heard White-Skin returning. "If you are well enough, sit
with me," Father said. "I have drawn a map of the rivers
to Johnson Hall that I want you to see."

Young-Wolf sat up quietly to look through the slit of
light at the curtain's edge. He could see the men sitting
side by side, their heads almost touching. They studied
the charcoal marks on the smooth bark slab. Father
pointed to the chain of rivers and lakes that linked
Ganundasaga to Fort Stanwix, the Mohawk River and,
eventually, Johnson Hall.

"I know these waters very well, and even with my
stiff knees, I can paddle. But you and Young-Wolf would
have to provide the real strength for the journey. There
are places where the canoe must be carried."

White-Skin sat back. "It is too much, my brother,
just to get me back into white man's country. Besides,

you must be here to take care of your family, your departed loved one's widow, and her little girl."

"I will take them along."

"It would not be safe," White-Skin protested as he held his head with his hands.

Father got up and walked to the fire. "What is safe in the life of a Seneca? And what is wrong with trying since Hawenio is the one who decides when we live and when we die?"

Father turned from the fire to look at White-Skin. Young-Wolf saw the other man raise his weary head to smile. "You have such a deep understanding of faith, Tekanondo. My own heart is encouraged to trust God because of your example." Then bowing low over the table, White-Skin grew silent.

Young-Wolf, his heart beating hard, stepped out into the room. "Father?" he ventured. "I am ready to do whatever I can to help save White-Skin-Brother's life."

Father's eyes were dark. "The strength of the bear is what we needed," he said harshly. "Our journey will remain nothing more than a dream if we do not get some food to strengthen our brother."

Young-Wolf dropped his head. "This is all my fault," he said, his voice starting to tremble. "And if White-Skin dies, I will be the one to blame." His eyes were drawn to White-Skin. A great weight of sorrow grew around Young-Wolf's neck as he saw the suffering he had caused.

White-Skin moved to unbutton the sleeves on his linen shirt. "Tekanondo," the man said. "I am thinking of something that might fill my belly. With your permission, perhaps I could ask Young-Wolf to trade my shirt for food."

"The nights are cold. You need your shirt." Father shook his head.

"I have the deerskin shirt our mother made me. I would do the trading myself if I had the strength." Father placed a hand on his brother's bent shoulders, as his eyes questioned Young-Wolf.

"I will do as White-Skin asks," Young-Wolf said with a solemn nod. "Somehow I will find the food he needs."

When White-Skin slipped the shirt over his head, Young-Wolf saw the pale flesh stretch over his rib cage. He handed the cloth to Young-Wolf. "If we *could* get to Johnson Hall, I know that Sir William would give us many supplies. We could bring these things back to stop the suffering in Ganundasaga."

"We?" Young-Wolf's father asked.

"Yes," White-Skin smiled. "Think of it. If we could stop this starving, there would be no reason for me to leave."

"After all you've been through, you would want to come back with us?" Young-Wolf asked.

"If it is Hawenio's will, that is exactly what I want to do."

Father patted White-Skin's back. "Truly you are friend and brother," he said. Then he raised his gaze to Young-Wolf. "If you succeed in getting food, my son, we can start looking for the tall elm tree tomorrow with which to make our canoe for the journey." There was bright hope in Father's eyes. "Within three days we could be on the river."

Young-Wolf stood taller. "I will go, Father. I will do my best, but before I leave, let me help White-Skin back into my bed."

White-Skin shook his head. "These are kind words, Young-Wolf, but I think I have enough strength to climb to the loft."

Young-Wolf looked down at the finely woven material in his hands. "This is your last piece of English clothing, isn't it?"

The man nodded with a slight grin.

"I am grateful . . . ," Young-Wolf paused. "I know you make this sacrifice because of me. . . . I am sorry for neglecting the trap and for the pain I caused."

Father gave a stern look. White-Skin-Brother smiled.

"Everyone except Hawenio himself fails to do right all the time, Young-Wolf," White-Skin said. "I can forgive you, Ha-ga, because I myself continually need forgiveness. Hawenio knows we are but dust. We fail, but he does not. When we are honest with our Creator, he has a way of turning even our weakness to strength. Now go, and the hand of Hawenio be on you."

It was raining again when Young-Wolf passed through the night to Bear-Lad's house. The door stood open, and he could see a young warrior with painted arms and a thin scalp lock melting lead for his shot mold beside the blue-flamed fire.

Just as Young-Wolf was ready to escape back in the darkness, the warrior looked up.

"Bear-Lad!" Young-Wolf gasped. "I didn't know you. You changed into a man overnight!"

Bear-Lad grinned. "Captain encourages me day by day. Soon I will be ready for battle."

Young-Wolf's knees grew weak. "Are you alone?" he asked, squeezing White-Skin's shirt to his chest and wondering if he could go on with his plan.

"Yes."

"Then I have a favor to ask of you." Young-Wolf made himself step inside. "I want to trade this for food."

Bear-Lad looked at the linen in his outstretched hand.

"I come to you because I know Captain and his men like English clothes," Young-Wolf explained quickly. "Besides this, I'm sure you know where they hide their stores. Bear-Lad, please. You helped by telling me about the trap. Now will you help me with this trade?"

Bear-Lad stood with his hands on his waist. "You speak as though you forget that *I* am one of Captain's men." He pulled the shirt from Young-Wolf's arm, taking time to look at Young-Wolf's bony wrists. "Is the food for the white man or for you?"

"For him, of course. I would not take his shirt to fill my stomach."

"Why do you want to keep him alive?"

Young-Wolf was silent.

"I know you too well," Bear-Lad said. "I have seen you go against the wishes of your grandfather and your father. If you did not really want to help this white man, no one could have forced you to come."

Young-Wolf avoided Bear-Lad's eyes. "This man is weak, but he shows no fear of things seen or unseen. . . . Doesn't it make sense to keep him alive long enough to understand why he is not afraid . . . even to die?"

Bear-Lad shook his head. "My heart is sorry for you. As the weakness of your family closes around you, you think less of strength. Remember the path we've traveled on. If you had not stopped for Samuel-Kirkland on the trail, you would have been one of Captain's men by now. Then strength, not death, would fill your mind."

"Will you trade the shirt for food or not?" Young-Wolf asked with a steady eye.

Bear-Lad reached into a basket by the fire. "Four ash cakes."

"That is all you will give for this shirt?"

"You want him just a little longer. Ask your questions now. These cakes will keep him alive a few more days." He smiled. "And when he's dead, Young-Wolf, tell me first. I know he has an English watch, and I would pay you in corn and venison for that."

"Then I will ask him now about the trade," Young-Wolf said hopefully.

But Bear-Lad squinted. "When he's *dead*," he said. "When he's dead."

In the rain Young-Wolf ran home with the bread under his shirt. Without a word to Father or Mother, he climbed the ladder. White-Skin was lying silently on his cornhusk mat, though the room still was lighted by a candle's tiny flame. Quickly Young-Wolf laid the small offering of food on the table and made haste to disappear.

"Young-Wolf, come here."

He turned to face the man rising from his bed. He watched White-Skin look over the food on the table. "I know I have failed," Young-Wolf blurted out. "Your shirt was worth more than four little loaves of bread."

But White-Skin shook his head. "You did not fail. You did as I asked. Four ash cakes are a great gift when the whole village is starving. Though your grandfather's men are good to me, I cannot think of one of them who would have four ash cakes to trade for a shirt."

"That's because they live as Senecas should," Young-Wolf replied. "No one has been hoarding. All have been sharing with brothers or cousins in need. But this is not so with Captain's people."

"You went to Captain's men? When they saw that it was my shirt, they still gave you food?"

"I went to Bear-Lad." He looked into the white man's eyes. "I told him I didn't want you to die . . . until I found out why you are not afraid of death."

White-Skin leaned over his table. He was silent for a long time. When he looked at Young-Wolf again, his eyes seemed happy. "I respect you very much. . . . And I thank you for what you have done." He handed one of the ash cakes back toward Young-Wolf.

Young-Wolf shook his head. "Those are all for you."

"Three days until we start our journey by canoe. One ash cake for each day. Is that enough for an Indian to live on?"

Young-Wolf nodded.

"Then with Hawenio's help, it will be enough for me. Take the other ash cake, if not for yourself, for your baby brother or Aunt's little girl."

Young-Wolf took the bread. He raised his eyes. "White-Skin . . . ? I should have told Bear-Lad that I did not want you to die because you are my brother . . . and because I have chosen you to be my friend."

8

WARNING OF THE LOONS

The next day the great elm tree was felled by two of Chief Old-Smoke's strongest men. Then Father taught White-Skin how to cut a ring below the lowest branches and make a slit down the entire length of the trunk. Once these lines were etched, Young-Wolf knew what to do. With the men, he pushed his own blunt hickory wedge under the bark to help peel the one huge sheet of skin away from the tree.

While they worked, Captain came to trouble them. "Tekanondo. First you take the bear out of season. Now you peel the bark before its time. You cannot free yourself from this English mind."

Young-Wolf's father ignored him, though the warrior came again and again. By the morning of the fourth day, the canoe, twice as tall as Father, was ready to be launched.

Captain came once more. This time he singled out Young-Wolf by the lakeshore. "I fear you have become the chickadee you once saw with Samuel-Kirkland. If you make this trip, you will be turning your back to Ganundasaga and following your stomach."

Young-Wolf continued putting his father's tools in order on the outstretched deerhide.

"Does it not concern you that in a few days you will go from a town of two white men and five hundred Senecas to a stone mansion where there will be only *six* Senecas in an entire settlement of palefaces?"

"*Seven* travel in this canoe, Captain," Young-Wolf said as he knelt to tie his knots around the tool pack. "Me, my father, my mother, my baby brother, my aunt and her little girl—*and* White-Skin-Brother. That makes *seven* Senecas. Did you miscount, or do you forget that Chief Old-Smoke has another son?"

"This journey is dangerous, Young-Wolf. You know nothing of the cruelty of white settlers. They have a saying, you know—the best Indian is a dead Indian." He raised his eyebrows. "And there are those who pay well for Indian headskins. Without a scalp lock you are good prey, Ha-ga. Some white fool will strip your skull, cut your hair in half, and have the pleasure of selling *two* Indian scalps. Now, I invite you to stay with me."

Young-Wolf stood, realizing that he was almost tall enough to look Captain in the eye. "Father cannot make this trip without me. You know that. Could it be that you do not want him to succeed with his plans? If we can bring supplies back to Ganundasaga, then the people will not starve. And they will know that White-Skin can be trusted to keep his word."

Captain turned on his heel. "Haa! You do not even know what Samuel-Kirkland will do once he reaches the safety of the forts. He may desert you, and without him, you will not have the manpower to come home on the waters."

"Then we will walk!" Young-Wolf huffed.

"You and Aunt could walk, but not the rest of your weak family. Is this what you really want, Young-Wolf— to be stranded in white man's territory?" He departed with a hostile grin.

Mother and Aunt with the little children in their arms came down to the sparkling water. Father and White-Skin each took an end of the canoe and waded waist-deep into the lake. Young-Wolf stayed on shore to hand them the long red-striped paddles and the supplies. The last to go in were his grinning little brother and shy, rabbit-eyed Little-Girl.

Father put Mother and Aunt in the middle with the children. Young-Wolf and White-Skin knelt on the floor near the bow. Father pushed off and took up his own seat in the back of the canoe. The morning lake breeze stroked Young-Wolf's cheeks as he looked back to the people left on shore. Grandfather and many men and women from the town shouted out their blessings. But Captain, Isaac, Bear-Lad, and a handful of warriors crossed their arms and walked away.

The next six days slipped by Young-Wolf like a dream. Enough fish gave themselves to Young-Wolf's spear to keep the travelers from starving. Paddling was easy since the water was high. They rode with the river currents from the outlet of Lake Ganundasaga to a gravel-shored island just inside the rim of the huge Oneida Lake. Here they made camp and waited for dawn. A sail through Oneida Lake, twenty miles long according to White-Skin's tongue, would take them close to Fort Stanwix, then the Mohawk River and finally Johnson Hall. The thought of tomorrow's adventures kept Young-Wolf awake half the night.

But in the morning, a sky as red as bloodroot sap met their eyes. Father tasted the dampness in the air. "A storm will brew in the kettle of rising wind by nightfall," he predicted. "We must start at once or risk being caught in the rain."

They broke camp without eating and hurriedly pushed off into deep water. Young-Wolf's father showed him how to drape a blanket over a pole and fix it on the mast to form a sail for the canoe. Then the three of them—White-Skin, Young-Wolf, and Father—paddled. The combination of wind and muscle-power pushed them across the water as smoothly as a gull in flight.

Still Father kept watching the sky. In the distance, loons moaned strange, weary sounds. White-Skin raised his head and listened, too. "Ot-kayason?" he asked, half jokingly to Father. This had been his first, most important phrase in Ganundasaga, and now he used it again.

But Father didn't smile. "They are loons, White-Skin, and there is great worry in the birds' calling."

As he spoke they were stabbed with a gust of chilly air. The lake began to lap around them like a pack of thirsty dogs. Quickly the women tied the supply packs to the exposed wood of the canoe frame. They hugged their children and turned their worried faces toward the gathering clouds.

Wind whistled in Young-Wolf's ears. The paddle, which had slipped like a knife through bear grease all morning and afternoon, fought him in the water. Rough walls of waves rose on every side. Soon they were rocking in a gale, their canoe no more stable than a sassafras root boiling in the kettle.

White-Skin reached up to grab the sail. The canoe tipped, throwing him face-first against the angry waves. Young-Wolf shouted at him, grabbed his belt and, with great difficulty, pulled him back inside. The man gulped in a series of urgent breaths, then put his paddle back into the water. He strained with Father to steer the boat toward shore.

"See the blockhouse . . . at the end of the lake. We must aim for there!" Father's shouting was frantic.

Rain pelted down. Aunt and Young-Wolf worked with cooking pots to keep the water from the boat. But for every toss they made, five splashes were spit back into the canoe by mounting, evil waves.

Father, anxious-eyed, handed his paddle to Young-Wolf. He worked his way to the mast. Pulling himself up, he took a stand against the whipping wind. From the squirrel-skin pouch that hung on his belt, he threw out two pinches of magic powder. "Do your best, O Wind. Pull hard, I say, but you will not be able to conquer us now."

Young-Wolf squeezed the paddle. If the magic worked, the serpents of the deep would soon breathe their last, roaring breaths.

But instead of turning belly-up in defeat, wind and water writhed together like a wounded gray-scaled monster. The canoe bow shot up into the air. Just as quickly it was slammed back down. The skin of elm exploded right between White-Skin's knees. With all his might, the man pushed the bundled blanket sail down to plug the hole.

Young-Wolf's father screamed, "White-Skin-Brother—pray!"

White-Skin yelled back at him. "I am praying! I am!"

Father wiped the rain from his eyes. "Well, I cannot hear your voice! Don't you see? We're drowning! Call out now! If your God's name be Jesus, let him hear your cry!"

White-Skin hugged the blanket at the bottom of the boat. "Lord God of the heavens! Thine name *is* Jesus Christ! Have mercy! Commander of wind and wave, hear my cry for help . . ."

The canoe spun like a twig caught in a creek. Soon Young-Wolf could not even guess their direction or distance from the shore. A violent jolt and a CRAACK ended their twisting course. The bark sheeting at the front of the boat ripped away from the framing wood, spewing Young-Wolf into dark water.

Gravel filled Young-Wolf's moccasins. It seemed too good to be true! He floundered to get a firm footing in the shallow water, while he saw White-Skin and Father wading toward the shore. They were towing the battered canoe that still held the women and Baby and Little-Girl.

White-Skin came running through the waves to reach for Young-Wolf's hand. "Thanks be to God, Haga, you're safe!" Young-Wolf gasped for strength and went to help them with the boat.

They sought the protection of some nearby pines, and when the rain had passed, they struggled to start a fire. Eventually there was a yellow light to huddle by. They were wet and miserable—but they were alive.

White-Skin sank down beside Young-Wolf near the blaze. The man stared at the fire so long that Father came to lay a hand on White-Skin's shoulder. "What is it, my brother? It seems that you lost your heart out there."

"We should not have come," White-Skin whispered. "We almost died."

Father pulled the man up with his wide strong hands. "But we did not perish," he answered. "Now look at me. The magic I have trusted in since youth proved useless today. But your God's Son Jesus Christ must be real. He heard and answered your voice."

White-Skin's eyes focused on Father. "Yes . . . truly, you are right." His face softened. "Ohh, I am very grateful to Jesus Christ our God." Suddenly the two men were half laughing and half crying together. "Ahh, my brother, we did almost enter heaven side by side," White-Skin said trembling. "But I am glad we're still here. Now that you believe Jesus Christ is Hawenio's Son, there is so much more you'll want to know."

The Book of Hawenio!" Father said. "I wonder if it's safe."

White-Skin hurried down to the shore, rummaged through the packs still tied inside the broken boat, and returned with the book in his hand. He sat down between Young-Wolf and his father.

"Back in Ganundasaga, you said your tongue stood ready to speak the words of Hawenio for us," Father said. "Is that same tongue ready now?"

White-Skin opened the book near the middle and struggled to separate the wet pages with his quivering hands. The breezes of dusk lifted his Seneca voice:

From heaven, Hawenio—the Lord—looks down
and sees all mankind;
from his dwelling place he watches
all who live on earth—
he who forms the hearts of all,
who considers everything they do.
No king is saved by the size of his army;
no warrior escapes by his great strength. . . .
But the eyes of the Lord—Hawenio—
are on those who fear him,
on those who put their hope in his unfailing love,
to deliver them from death
and keep them alive in famine.
We wait in hope for Hawenio—the Lord;
he is our help and our shield.
In him our hearts rejoice,
for we trust in his holy name.

Mother and Aunt drew the children closer to the fire. Mother cleared her throat. "I want to hear what your book says about Jesus," she said softly. "Even though Hawenio brought us out of the water, I feel black hands of death coming after me." Her eyes were weary and swollen as she struggled to speak more. ". . . and I need to know who this Jesus, giver of peace, is." A cough as violent as the storm cut her off. Father hurried for a half-dry blanket to put around her shoulders. When she grew quiet again, she nodded. "I listen, my brother . . . truly I must know . . ."

White-Skin looked at her tenderly. Then he turned the thin pages. "These are some of Hawenio's words about his Son—'Jesus Christ is the exact likeness of the unseen God. He existed before God made anything at all. . . . He was before all else began and it is his power that holds everything together.'"

Tekanondo lifted his hands toward the purple sky. "We have seen this power," he said. "And we give thanks to you, Hawenio, for it."

"Amen!" White-Skin spoke this English word as he, too, raised his arms. Then he looked into the book again. "It was through what Hawenio's Son did that Hawenio cleared a path for everything to come to him—all things in heaven and on earth—for the death of the Son on the cross has made peace with Hawenio for all by his blood."

"What is this cross?" Young-Wolf asked as he turned his wet back toward the fire. "And how can the book speak of the Son of Hawenio's having blood as I do?"

White-Skin smiled. "You have good questions, Haga. I will try to answer clearly." He closed his eyes. "Christ is the perfection and beauty of Hawenio himself. Yet he laid aside these treasures to become a man—with flesh and blood—like yours and mine. Those same hands that set the stars in place also came to touch the sick and downhearted on this earth."

Mother's cough opened White-Skin's eyes. "You spoke of Christ's death," she said. "This means that even the Maker of Life has died? How, then, is it possible to find peace in him?"

"Christ chose to die," White-Skin said steadily. "That was Hawenio's plan. Blood is the payment for sin, and because we all fall short of his perfection, someone must die to pay for our wrongdoing. Otherwise, no one could hope to know Hawenio at all."

"And Hawenio let his own Son die for us?" Tekanondo asked with his hands on his knees.

"His own Son," White-Skin agreed. "Jesus allowed himself to be born of a virgin woman in a small town called Bethlehem of Judea. Every moment of his life, Jesus listened to the Great Good Voice and did his father's will. But instead of being grateful for the wonder of coming face-to-face with God himself, people cursed the name of Jesus, tortured him, and killed him by nailing his hands and feet to a cross made out of trees."

"Then he is dead," Mother's voice shook.

"He died," White-Skin said with a gentle smile, "but he is not dead. Truly the Evil One and all the wicked spirits of the world rejoiced when Jesus Christ was laid into the grave. But three days after his burial he came to life again, proving that he has power over all evil and death. This is our peace. If we believe Jesus died for us, he stands ready to raise us from our graves. We need not fear anything because Christ himself will keep us safe in death."

"You speak good words, my brother," Mother said with a contented sigh. "I believe each one of them."

White-Skin smiled. "Then living or dying, Sister, you belong to God. And nothing will divide you from Hawenio's love." Aunt put her arm around Mother's shoulder while Father studied the firelight dancing on White-Skin's face.

"This was a great sacrifice of friendship that God made for you and me," Father said. "White-Skin-Brother, I begin to see why you suffered so many moons of sorrow to bring Hawenio's book to my family and to me."

"Tekanondo, I have endured so little compared with Christ's sufferings." White-Skin eyes were wet. "He is the one who teaches love. He is the one who encourages us to give our lives for each other." He looked at Young-Wolf. "You have seen my weaknesses. Now, praise God, you have seen his strength."

"From this night on, we walk as those who have promised their friendship to Hawenio himself," Father said.

"And may the God of Peace—who raised Jesus from the dead—give us strength to fulfill this promise," White-Skin replied.

Suddenly Mother doubled over. At the end of her violent coughs blood flowed from her lips.

White-Skin jumped to his feet. "I am going to get help. That blockhouse can't be too far away."

"I will go with you," Young-Wolf said, his eyes wide with worry because of Mother.

But White-Skin touched his arm. "Your father might need your help tonight," he said. "I promise I'll be back as quickly as I can."

9

FISH WITH SHARP TEETH

A bright-faced sun crept up over the pines to wake Young-Wolf the next morning. He rose stiffly from the damp ground. Baby cried, and he saw that Mother was too weak to reach for him. Choking back a sob, he watched her labored breathing as she lay by the powdery ashes of last night's fire.

Father walked to him, his hand resting on the metal tomahawk in his belt. "Do you hear, Young-Wolf? It is the step of horses."

Now that Father had turned his ear toward the sound, Young-Wolf did hear hoofbeats and a jingle of metal, too.

"It will be well if it is our brother," Father said, pressing his sheathed hunting knife into Young-Wolf's hand. "But if it is someone else, it might mean danger."

Young-Wolf followed his father to the edge of the pines.

"Pull up here, Sir."

Young-Wolf did not understand the odd words drifting through the trees, but he knew the voice—it was

White-Skin-Brother's. Young-Wolf was ready to go to him, but Father held him back. "Be cautious. You can never tell what will happen in white man's country."

He searched his father's face. "You are like Captain," he whispered. "You don't trust White-Skin here."

"It is not White-Skin. It is the man with White-Skin," his father answered as a wagon driven by an English officer pulled into the clearing. White-Skin jumped down from the wagon seat and ran to them.

"How is Sister?" he asked anxiously.

Father shook his head. "Weaker than ever."

White-Skin lowered his eyes. "I am sorry it took me so long. I ate some rice and venison with the officer before we started back."

Young-Wolf's teeth gritted together, but Father squeezed White-Skin's wrist. "You needed the food. There is no need for being sorry."

White-Skin dug into the sack he carried. "Here, eat. There are biscuits and pieces of salt pork." He filled Father's hands. Then he gave the bag to Young-Wolf. "Feed everyone," he said. "It is food . . . real food to eat."

Young-Wolf ran to Aunt and the two children on her lap. "Look." Young-Wolf smiled at them. "Look, it's food."

Aunt gently pushed the little ones off her knees. She piled meat and biscuits into her lap. "We are grateful, Ha-ga. Now that you have taken care of us, you eat."

Young-Wolf turned to the pines. He sat down at the edge of the woods to fill his belly. The dry English bread could not reach his stomach fast enough. He stuffed his mouth, realizing he had not eaten anything in more than two days. Even before he had finished chewing, hunger made him search for more. But the bag was empty, so he started eating precious crumbs that had fallen to the ground.

The round-bellied English officer, in his flaming red coat, came to stare at him. His roaring laugh shook the air as he watched Young-Wolf sort through the pine needles and dirt looking for the last bites of bread. White-Skin came running. The officer spoke happy English words, but the anger in White-Skin's face cut his speaking off.

"Why is he laughing?" Young-Wolf asked. "Has *he* never been hungry?"

White-Skin let a sigh slide through his teeth. "It is not worth worrying about, Ha-ga. But after this, stay closer to your father or me. Now come help us load the supplies and canoe into the wagon. I know a place where we can go to rest and mend our canoe."

English-Officer impatiently twitched the ends of the leather reins against his wrist as he watched their work from his driver's seat. Finally when the canoe, supplies, women, and children had been loaded onto the wagonbed, English-Officer motioned for Father and White-Skin to sit up front with him. White-Skin agreed, but Father pushed his tomahawk securely into his belt. By this action and the tilt of his head he showed he was ready to walk.

The Englishman shook his head as he eyed Young-Wolf. Young-Wolf copied his father's moves, though the hunting knife at his waist seemed a small sign of power compared with Father's deadly weapon. Slowly they followed the two brown horses and wagon down the rutted road. The strong sun drew the dampness of last night's rain up around their feet. As they plodded on throughout the day, Young-Wolf's heart swelled with admiration for his father. He knew the man's legs ached. Still he walked.

Finally they stopped at an English house. A woman in full bright skirts that brushed the ground came out to greet them. White-Skin jumped from the wagon to give her hand a gentle, enthusiastic squeeze. He spoke both English and the Six-Nation tongue of the Oneidas to her. Young-Wolf's eyes widened with questions. "White or Indian, Father—which is she?"

Perhaps White-Skin had overheard him, since he brought the woman up to them. "This is Sarah Montour, half-sister to my friend Skenondon of the Oneidas. Tekanondo, she invites us to bring your wife to rest in her home."

But before Father would move Mother, he strode through the cool dark house. He eyed the high beds stuffed with colorful blankets, while Young-Wolf gazed at the pictures, plates, and mirrors on the walls. "She will be fine here," the woman assured them with Oneida words.

Father grunted as though he doubted. Still he carried Mother in and laid her on the bed. Mother coughed violently, then fell back to sleep. Aunt and the children followed Father in. Baby started coughing, too, and Sarah-Montour looked into the little boy's eyes. She frowned and spoke slow words to Aunt that Young-Wolf did not take time to understand. He only wanted to be outside.

In the light shade of a maple with newly born leaves Father mixed elm powder paste to seal the seams of the canoe. Young-Wolf squatted near him, beside the broken boat which now sat on grass. With new strips of hickory lashings, brought for just such an emergency, Young-Wolf fixed the seams. Near dusk Aunt joined him, skillfully tying the knots to finish his work. "How is Mother now?" he asked.

"As she always is, my child," Aunt replied with more than her usual few words. "Who but Hawenio knows the number of her days?"

Young-Wolf sucked in his grief. Aunt was so much better than he when it came to facing death.

After a full supper with meat and bread, Aunt and the children stayed inside to sleep. But Young-Wolf, White-Skin, and Father went back to the maple tree.

"I cannot help but think of white men as hungry, sharp-toothed fish," Father said with heavy words. "All along our trail today I saw cows and plowed fields and chickens, where our people once roamed. Nothing remains of Indian land. The English have come up the Mohawk River to eat all of the little Six-Nation fish."

A fingernail of moon had scratched its way into the black sky. By its light Young-Wolf saw White-Skin nodding, as the man rested his chin on his knees.

"Oh, there are traces of Indian life," Father went on, "little pieces—like the Oneida words spoken here. Yet, I am sure that even these are valued no more than fishbones after the feast is done."

"Your words are true," White-Skin replied. "I do not know what to say to comfort you."

105

Father watched the moon. "Hawenio and his Son Jesus can sit beyond the skies, but what are we to do when our feet are stuck in clay?"

White-Skin grabbed Father's arms. "You have spoken strength to me in these many months when I lived with you among the Senecas. Now that you are here with me among the white men, let me be the tongue that speaks to you. Do not give up, my Tekanondo—" His voice shook with emotion. "Do not give up. Even here, your saying is true. Hawenio in every deed must do as he pleases. We must look for God's way. . . . Because we are friends, we can look together."

Tekanondo took White-Skin's hand and formed a strong fist over it. "Then we stay committed to each other," he said. "Whether among Indians or whites, we will call each other friend."

"Yes," White-Skin promised. "I pledge myself to you."

Both men looked to Young-Wolf. "My son, are you willing to make this pledge with us?" Father asked.

Young-Wolf hesitated. "I do not know. The path you speak of is as dim as a forest trail on a moonless night." He pulled at the damp grass. "I cannot see far enough to tell what it is like, and I would not choose a path I could not see."

"We cannot see the trail of life," Father told him. "One step ahead of where we now are, and the future is hidden around the bend. But I see truth even when I cannot see the trail. If we choose our traveling companions well, my son, we need not fear even the darkest path. I have trusted White-Skin, and he has led me to trust in Hawenio's Son, his good Friend."

The closeness of tears suddenly stung Young-Wolf's eyes. He blinked as he looked at White-Skin-Brother. "My hand moves from my heart," he said, choosing his words carefully. "I have heard many words from the Book of Hawenio now, and I welcome them all. I will walk with you and Father even on a thorny trail."

Both White-Skin and his father beamed with pride. "What good words!" his father said.

"It is well." White-Skin nodded. "Now Hawenio can have his way with all of us."

Five days later the mended canoe brought Young-Wolf's family safely to land that was familiar to White-Skin's eyes. They carried the boat out of the river and rested for a short while. Then they started a tiresome journey overland. When the sun stood high in the sky, they finally broke away from the pale green woodlands. Their eyes were cheered by row upon row of apple trees in bloom.

Father let Mother sink down into the long grass underneath the fragrant branches, while Young-Wolf and White-Skin put down the canoe. Young-Wolf, his shoulders numb from the walk, threw himself onto the warm fresh earth. White-Skin stretched out beside him. "Thanks be to God," the man said, slipping into his English tongue. Then in Seneca he prayed, "Hawenio, I am grateful that you have brought us to the edges of Johnson Hall."

Young-Wolf squinted in the sunlight. "Are we that close?" he said, his heart beating with relief.

"About five English miles." White-Skin smiled. "This orchard is owned by Wemple-the-Blacksmith's people. Beyond this land lies Sir William's property."

Father sat down with them. "I would like to stay under these trees, my brother. Their flowers cheer my wife's sick heart. I do not want to go to Johnson Hall."

White-Skin sat up to look at him, lines of tiredness spreading out like sunrays from his eyes. "All right. I will see what I can do."

By nightfall Father and Young-Wolf had built a hut with the bark and wood and straw White-Skin gathered from the Wemples and their neighbors. Father, with hardly enough strength to move his swollen knees, carried Mother through the low doorway of their temporary home. He put her where she could see the blossoms through the square smoke hole in the roof.

Aunt and the children came inside the pine-scented shelter. They carried smiles on their faces and pots that overflowed with gifts of food. As Aunt laid her first fire in the new house, she laughed. "It would be wrong to cook all pots at once—but what a joy to try."

They ate a celebration meal in peace, and the next day Young-Wolf followed White-Skin on the path to Johnson Hall. The Indian agent's huge stone house loomed before them like a gray square-eyed giant sunning himself in the center of wide-open space. Long-legged horses roamed in fields that stretched as far as the eye could see.

White-Skin knocked at the door. Almost at once a huge, wide-chested Englishman greeted them. He was dressed in a lacy shirt and brown knee-length breeches with white stockings and buckled shoes. Young-Wolf's eyes fastened on the mass of stiff, white hair that fell around the Englishman's face.

Grinning ear to ear with surprise, he pulled White-Skin inside. "Mister Kirkland!" he shouted, going on with other English words.

White-Skin stood with him in the wide white room just inside the door. Soon he came back out for Young-Wolf. "This is Young-Wolf, my Wolf Clan brother," White-Skin said in Seneca. "He is Old-Smoke's grandson and Tekanondo's elder child."

The Man-with-False-White-Hair grinned. To Young-Wolf's surprise, he spoke Seneca clearly. "Greetings. I am Wolf Clan, too. But look closely or you see only a middle-aged Irishman. My adopted people are Mohawks. I give thanks to you for looking after Mister Kirkland so very well."

Young-Wolf's voice should have spoken now, but it did not.

False-Hair pulled at the white cuffs that hid his wrists from view. "Come with me," he said to Young-Wolf. "I have something you will like."

He led them into a bright room with blue designs drawn on every wall. From the smooth table there False-Hair took a white dish filled with dark stones. "Is this your first time away from Ganundasaga?" False-Hair asked.

Young-Wolf managed to nod.

"Then you will be delighted to taste one of these." He almost pressed the plate into Young-Wolf's chest.

Young-Wolf's eyes ran to White-Skin's.

"It's all right." His elder brother smiled. "Those are called choc-o-lates. But be careful—eat only one. Remember, we were starving yesterday. We must give our bodies time."

Starving—the word, the whole experience seemed distant now. It was hard for Young-Wolf's mind to walk back through time to think of it as his tongue rolled the delicious sweetness inside his mouth.

"I can see you have won the respect of the people," False-Hair said. "This boy's family would not let him travel alone with you if they did not trust you."

"Tekanondo waits at the shelter he has built in Wemple's orchard," White-Skin explained. "I will state my business and then we must go back there."

False-Hair raised his eyebrows. "Sit down, Mister Kirkland. I wish to hear what you have to say."

White-Skin dusted off the seat of his skin pants and sat down on one of the thin-legged chairs that ringed the table. Young-Wolf, following his example, brushed off the back of his breechcloth and plopped down on the seat next to White-Skin. False-Hair's eyes danced with laughter, and Young-Wolf, feeling foolish, looked away.

"I pray you've gotten the letters I've been sending you," White-Skin said to the other man. "I wrote every one of them in the presence of the chief and the council so that they would know my exact words to you. My brothers, Sir, are eager for aid, and indeed they need it desperately."

False-Hair pursed his lips. He started speaking in English, but White-Skin stopped him. "For the sake of the chief's grandson, I ask you to keep your speech in Seneca. He is old enough to consider your thoughts."

The man put his fingers together. "Let's just say, Mister Kirkland, that Indians often think we Englishmen are ankle-deep in riches. Rarely do they consider the King's expenses in giving such gifts."

"And Indians are up to their necks in sorrow!" White-Skin raged. "Rarely do Englishmen think of this!"

"Truly," False-Hair answered, "but few of them would even care." He studied White-Skin's face. "You are thin as a whipping post. I can see it has been hard for you. In fact I am amazed you have survived. Murders between Indians and whites take place every day. It was wise for you to ask your Indians to bring you home."

"I did not ask. Tekanondo, my brother, insisted. I was starving. That, Sir, is the nature of things in Ganundasaga. That is why Young-Wolf comes with me. We want the supplies you can give us. Then we will go home."

"Mister Kirkland, you're not serious. You risk your life in Seneca country."

"Hawenio is my life." White-Skin smiled. "I take my instructions from him."

"We'll talk tomorrow," False-Hair said, rising to his feet. "I'll tell the servants to make up a room—"

"No, thank you." White-Skin pushed back his chair. "We will walk back and forth from Wemple's every day until we have gathered the supplies we need. You see, my sister is close to death with consumption."

"Indeed. Even the kindest of neighbors will not understand why you live in an Indian's hut. What will you say to them?"

"That the coldness of my love would dishonor my great and holy God if I deserted my family now." White-Skin looked out the window. "I am not the same man you sent to Ganundasaga, Sir William. I have Seneca family now, and I may never be able to live a white man's life again."

False-Hair showed them to the door. He shook White-Skin's hand. "I admire you, Mister Kirkland. At the same time, I could say you are a fool."

At the end of the long trail home Young-Wolf slipped through the doorway to their hut, White-Skin at his heels. Father greeted them with wet, red eyes. "It's Mother!" Young-Wolf gasped, sorrow grabbing at his throat.

Father nodded. "She died in peace. . . . And Baby, too." He blinked. "It was as though she waited until she knew death could be safe . . ." Father's voice broke as White-Skin's arms fell around his neck. Tears streamed down both men's faces. Father went on, ". . . I know from the way she died . . . that Hawenio's Son was here. He did not let her go alone."

Young-Wolf pushed himself outside. A bird sang. The blossoms filled the air with sweetness—but nothing was as real as his aching grief.

10

THE RIVER HOME

Every stroke of the oar widened the distance between Young-Wolf's family and the two freshly dug graves left behind in Wemple's orchard. Each dip into the water pulled at the aches in Young-Wolf's muscles and the pain in his heart. Their course was set toward Ganundasaga after almost a full month of collecting supplies at Johnson Hall.

Now they rowed into Oneida Lake in a small bateau, the only vessel False-Hair had been able to give them. It was a wide, flat-bottomed boat designed by white men to transport white men's supplies. Aunt took the rudder, the flesh on her face wrinkled with exhaustion, but her eyes sharp with determination. To pass the time, Little-Girl sat at her feet and picked at the weaving in her mother's cornhusk moccasins.

Young-Wolf and White-Skin rowed near the front of the boat, shoulder to shoulder with their bare backs toward the water. In the center sat Father. His oar stayed dry, his eyes wet, for mile upon English mile.

The stare of the sun, the biting mosquitoes, the

sweat in their eyes showed no mercy for their sorrows. At night they camped on shore. By day they pressed on without Father's help.

"When will he row?" Young-Wolf moaned to White-Skin after days on the water. Already they had come through Oneida Lake, Three Rivers, and down into Seneca waters. "My hands burn with blisters. Swimming waters fill my head."

"It is his time of mourning," White-Skin answered. "We must pray and be patient. Soon we will be at the Long Falls, and then we must have his help." White-Skin pulled out a long pole from the bottom of the boat. "The water is shallow here. I will push us upstream for a while. You take a rest."

That same afternoon they passed through the still, swampy waters at the mouth of Cayuga Lake. The sun started walking down the sky as they paused below the first set of rapids. White-Skin put his hand on Father's back. "Tekanondo—I worry about getting this boat up between the rocks at Long Falls," he said. "It is no slim Indian canoe. I need your skill and your strength."

Father looked up as though waking from a week-long dream. "We'll need both oars and pole," he said, suddenly speaking with a voice of command.

White-Skin smiled. "I knew—with Hawenio's help—you would see us through, my brother."

"I have never steered this kind of boat," Father said, lifting his voice above the sound of the water. "But we will bend our wills as one and try."

White-Skin sighed gratefully as he sat down next to Young-Wolf. They put in their oars. Now Father, the tall dark-skinned warrior, manned the pole. As the boat moved along, it gave off little growls whenever it scraped over hidden rocks. Aunt put Little-Girl in the center of the barrels of corn, cloth, and ammunition. Then she moved to the front to help set a course. "Rock there . . . logs . . . too narrow." Like a nervous catbird she squawked.

Father bore his eyes into the water as he gripped the pole. Young-Wolf and White-Skin kept their faces to his and pulled with all their might. Suddenly they were trapped by rock.

"Hold up!" Father yelled. He pulled up the pole and let the boat turn downstream with the current. "Again!" he shouted. Young-Wolf saw him grind his teeth as he looked for a wider space. They made some progress. Then the boat jerked to a halt.

"Young-Wolf," Father shouted. "Look over the edges. This time I can't see where we are snagged."

"I can't tell either!" Young-Wolf called back as he bowed over the swirling waters.

White-Skin threw down his oar. "I'm going in," he said. "Maybe I can find it and push us off."

Aunt's eyes grew wide with fear as White-Skin splashed overboard. He floundered in the quick, chest-deep water.

"I see it!" he said triumphantly, putting a shoulder to the vessel. "Back up! There! Right—now!" He flopped like a fish out of harm's way as Father managed to move the boat again.

White-Skin clung to the side, his knuckles white against the wet wood. "That worked well. I'll stay in the water."

A moment later, they faced the same trial again.

After that rock another came, and another, until White-Skin-Brother was gasping for breath at the boat's edge. "Young-Wolf, go in with him," Father said. "You see what he is doing. I think you are strong enough." Without a moment's hesitation, Young-Wolf dropped into the chilly waters. His bare feet gripped the slippery stones. White-Skin smiled. "Welcome—Creek-Wader!"

"Truly, Water-Biter!" Young-Wolf teased back.

Together they made good progress for a while. "Probably only seven more miles to go," White-Skin panted when fatigue made them take a break.

"Again!" Father encouraged them. "If we don't move on, darkness will trap us here."

Young-Wolf blew out the little remaining air from his chest.

"Go!" Father said, leaning into the pole.

The boat answered back with a sickening scrape.

"Whoa! Whoa!" White-Skin shouted. He motioned for Young-Wolf to press his back against the side. Then putting his shoulder to the boat, he grimaced as he pushed with all his might. "We've—got—to get it—off from here."

Suddenly unseen rocks jarred free.

"Ho-hoo!!!" Father yelled out above them.

But Young-Wolf screamed. "My leggg . . . it's trapped!" He whirled in pain as White-Skin grabbed him. "Have mercy, Jesus!" the man cried as the boat swung back, freeing Young-Wolf to be lifted up by White-Skin's quivering arms.

Aunt and Father peered over the side. Now that he was out of danger Young-Wolf found his courage again, though the water slashed his wound. Leaning into White-Skin for support, he brought his leg out of the river. "Look," he managed, his sight half-blackened with pain. "It's only a cut. . . . I can move my ankle and my knee."

His blood swirled with the current as Father's hand pulled him into the boat. Young-Wolf pinched his flesh to slow the bleeding, while Aunt brought a strip of new calico from a supply pack to tie up his leg.

"I'll go in again," Young-Wolf volunteered once he proved to himself that he could walk.

"It is no use. We are stuck in both front and back," Father moaned. "Besides, White-Skin is so tired that he cannot go on." Father threw down his pole and pulled his brother into the boat. White-Skin, exhausted, dropped to the floor. Father slid beside him, holding both swollen knees.

"I will run to Ganundasaga!" Young-Wolf announced.

Father looked at Young-Wolf. "You could never make it, my son."

"I must try," Young-Wolf said, already climbing over the side. His eye caught White-Skin's. "Speak to Hawenio for me." Then he splashed toward the bank, and using roots, he pulled himself to shore.

Young-Wolf hopped along through the open woods until he came to the Six-Nations Trail. Already he was dragging his injured leg. The air was warm, but his body shivered with worry and pain. On and on and on he went through the green-gray forest, with Brother Sun racing him toward town. There were times when the pain dulled, and he could hardly remember his reason for limping. And there were times when his mind dulled, and he could hardly remember his reason for running.

Finally the land seemed more familiar. He knew the cornfields of Ganundasaga were near. With each stabbing breath, a prayer drummed in his ears. "I need your strength, Hawenio. I need your strength to go on." But suddenly the words dried on his thirsty tongue. The sweat running into his eyes turned the forest black. When his vision cleared again, he found himself lying in the middle of the trail.

"Son of Hawenio . . . help me!" His words were almost cut off by grief. "I have to make it home." Struggling to raise his head, he saw the sun falling slowly through the treetops. Ganundasaga could not be that far away. Still he had no strength to go on.

"Goo-weh! . . . Goo-weh! . . . Goo-weh!" His voice carried the distress call of his people down the trail. "Goo-weh! Goo-weh! Goo-weh!" he cried out again and again.

Suddenly the chief's swift messenger was running toward him on the path. The strong man swooped over him, pulled him up, and grasped his wrists to lift Young-Wolf onto his back. But Young-Wolf protested. "No! Go home fast! Tell the chief that his sons are stuck in Long Falls! Then come back for me."

The warrior nodded, let him down gently, and dashed away. Young-Wolf, sobbing with pain and relief, pushed himself to the edge of the trail. He found a cushion of dead leaves piled high underneath some fragrant saplings, and there under the cover of the forest he immediately drifted into a dark, but contented, sleep.

An early evening sky met Young-Wolf when he opened his eyes. Cool water from a bowl touched his lips. "Bear-Lad," he breathed. "How did you find me?"

"Outside the council house, I heard the messenger talk to your grandfather. When all the chief's men were sent down along the river, I decided to come to you. I did not want you to be alone."

Young-Wolf struggled to keep himself alert. "How long have I been here?"

"I have been beside you since the sun touched the land. How long you were here before that, I do not know."

"The supplies from the river?" Young-Wolf asked.

"They have been carried right past you, while you slept here in the woods." Bear-Lad smiled. "And just a few moments ago, Aunt and her little girl also walked by you on the trail. I was silent in the dusk, and no one noticed us."

"And Father? And White-Skin?"

"They come more slowly. After their day in the river, I am sure they are very tired." A storm seemed to brew in Bear-Lad's eyes.

"What are you thinking?" Young-Wolf's heart started racing. "Where is Captain?"

"Come." Bear-Lad stood up. "I will take you to your grandfather's house."

"Answer me!" Young-Wolf demanded as he sat up painfully. "I can see you have dark thoughts. Where is Captain?"

"You are not one of Captain's men. I do not have to tell you everything."

"It *is* Captain then who troubles you. Is it because he plans more evil against White-Skin-Brother?"

"Why should you care?" Bear-Lad glared at him.

"I have overheard the news here on this trail. Your mother and brother are dead. These deaths are Samuel-Kirkland's fault."

"No. My white brother speaks of peace, not death," Young-Wolf argued. "Take me down the trail to Father. Then you will understand. I will explain things as we go."

"I will not lead you into danger," Bear-Lad argued. "I will take you home."

Young-Wolf pushed himself to stand on his good leg. "I am going to find White-Skin and Father."

Bear-Lad eyed him. "You will not even make it to the trail."

Young-Wolf shut his eyes against the pain. "Son of Hawenio, have mercy," he breathed, remembering White-Skin's most desperate plea. Though his leg felt tortured with fire, he reached the trail. Young-Wolf limped toward the river while Bear-Lad followed him, as though the other boy didn't know what to do.

Just then an owl hooted. Young-Wolf squinted. "That is one of Captain's men, isn't it?"

"Do not go back to the river!" Bear-Lad ordered. "Then I know you will be safe."

Young-Wolf looked into his face. "I must warn Father. Captain does plan to do White-Skin harm!"

The hoot came again. "I must go," Bear-Lad's voice shook as he pulled himself away. "But you stay here!" Young-Wolf watched the boy disappear into the dark woods ahead of him. Hesitating for only a moment, Young-Wolf continued on the trail. "Father! Be careful!" he shouted out with all his strength. "Captain is waiting for White-Skin!"

Suddenly hands were on Young-Wolf's throat. Captain silenced him by pressing one palm against his nose and mouth. "So now you limp even as your father and White-Skin have done in the past," Captain whispered harshly. "Doesn't this evil teach you anything? How can you want to save this white man from the punishment he deserves?"

Young-Wolf trembled, but Captain would not remove his hand to let him speak. "I know about your mother and your baby brother. Surely now Tekanondo will give this murderous White-Skin into my hands."

Young-Wolf struggled to shake his head.

Captain's grip grew tighter. "We will see," he said with a satisfied grin. "I plan to meet them right here on the trail. If your father is foolish enough to disagree with me, I will use what means I have to change his mind. My men are everywhere, awaiting my commands."

Even as Captain spoke, Young-Wolf saw the warrior Isaac slip from hiding. Except for his breechcloth, he was naked, and when he neared them, Young-Wolf noticed that his face was painted black and red for war.

Captain held Young-Wolf firmly while Isaac loaded his rifle. Soon, at Captain's nod, all three of them walked out onto the trail, right in front of White-Skin and Young-Wolf's father. The sky was still light enough for Young-Wolf to see the surprise on the tired men's faces. As Captain spoke, Young-Wolf finally shook himself free.

"Tekanondo, your wife and baby are dead because of this man. Now, for their sakes, we will send him to his grave."

Father stared steadily at Captain. "Because of this man, my wife and baby are at peace now. If he had not come and endured with us in Ganundasaga, they would have died in fear." Father looked to Isaac, who cradled the rifle in his arm. "Let us pass unharmed."

"You may go to Ganundasaga, Brother," Captain said. "But not this white man."

Young-Wolf wrung his hands as Isaac leveled his gun at White-Skin-Brother's shoulders. Immediately Father put himself between his brother and Isaac's gun. "This man is still my father's adopted son." Father raised his voice. "He risked his life to bring food back to our people. If you disagree with him, come to council tomorrow and give light to your thoughts. That is how Seneca brothers disagree."

"You are as white as your *white* brother," Captain shouted, "or you would not defend him."

Father stood his ground. "I was born Seneca. I will die Seneca. I am the vessel Hawenio has made. Only he may choose my path for me. We are going back to Ganundasaga, Captain. Stand aside."

Young-Wolf, his head pounding, hobbled over to Father. "My son." Father's strong voice was suddenly broken by his even stronger feelings. "I am grateful to see you again." He pulled Young-Wolf's arm around his shoulder to take the weight from his injured leg. And while Isaac watched in silence, White-Skin slowly moved to take up Young-Wolf's other arm.

"Come with us," Father said, and though Young-Wolf's injury slowed their pace, they soon had their backs toward both Captain and Isaac.

"Hawenio in every deed must do as he pleases," Father whispered to give them courage.

Still fear turned Young-Wolf's head to look back. Isaac was squeezing the trigger. "Father—he's going to shoot!"

At the same moment a dull-sounding snap came through the dusk. Just as suddenly Captain and Isaac bolted from the trail. Then they heard the sound of many feet running deep into the woods.

White-Skin found his voice. "The gun—it misfired!" he cried. "Praise God!" Father closed his eyes and grasped Young-Wolf's quaking hand. The forest wrapped them in silence.

Instead of going into town, they made their way to Ganundasaga Lake, where the waters still held some fading light from the sky. Sitting on the shore, they gazed in silence. Father touched Young-Wolf's shoulder. "Will you be all right if we stay here tonight?"

Young-Wolf felt the smile growing deep within. "I am sore and tired, Father, but I feel very well."

"So do I," Father answered, looking into his eyes. "This very night, my son, I saw you grow into a warrior. My heart is raised up because of you."

He then turned to White-Skin-Brother.

"We have laid thorns across our old trails, my friend. You are not the same Samuel-Kirkland who walked to us when the earth slept under the snows. And we are not the same Senecas who greeted you by that first council fire. Though we are not understood by our

own people now, I do not think of us as men without nation or cause."

"Truly," White-Skin grinned wearily, "let Hawenio choose our real homes."

"We will go to council tomorrow and talk with Captain there," Father decided. "From the words of that meeting, we can weave our plans." Father dug into the small pack he had carried with him. He put the Book of Hawenio into White-Skin's hand. "Let the words of Hawenio strengthen us for this new way."

White-Skin shook his head. "It is too dark to see the words, Tekanondo, but I will speak out of those already written in my heart."

Looking out across the waters, he began, "Hawenio says, 'I will not leave you as orphans. I will come to you. . . . Because I live, you also will live. On that day you will realize that I am in my Father, and you are in me, and I am in you. Whoever hears my commands and obeys them, he is the one who loves me. . . . And greater love has no man than this, that one lay down his life for his friends.' "

126

Historical Note

The adventures in *River of Danger* are based on facts from *The Journals of Samuel Kirkland: 18th-Century Missionary to the Iroquois, Government Agent, Father of Hamilton College,* ed. Walter Pilkington (Clinton, N.Y.: Hamilton College, 1980).

In February 1765, Samuel Kirkland walked more than one hundred miles with Indian scouts from Johnson Hall—still standing in Johnstown, New York—to Ganundasaga near today's Geneva, New York. Because of land pressures and conflicts in lifestyles, the hatred between Indians and whites in his time was very real. That he survived and that Tekanondo truly became his friend are testimonies to God's love and Samuel Kirkland's dedication to his Indian family.

Continual hardships and threats on his life finally caused Kirkland to leave Ganundasaga in May 1766. Tekanondo accompanied him on his travels that summer. Together they appeared before the Connecticut General Assembly. Tekanondo also attended Kirkland's ordination at Eleazar Wheelock's school and did some work with Kirkland to prepare others for living among the Iroquois. According to the records of Samson Occom, Wheelock's first Indian pupil, Tekanondo's son attended Wheelock's school in 1768.

For the next forty years, Kirkland lived and worked among the Oneidas. During the whirlwinds of the American Revolutionary War, the Continental Congress relied on his understanding of Indian language and culture. Though some Oneida and Tuscarora Indians maintained their neutrality, Chief Old-Smoke and many other Iroquois warriors sided with the British. In the end few American or European leaders showed concern that the unity of the Six Nations Iroquois Confederacy was being destroyed by the seeds sown in this war.

Despite the tragedies they faced, the Indian people Kirkland served continued to look upon him as an honest, faithful friend. His journal entries in June 1788 record a return visit to the shores of Ganundasaga Lake. That time perhaps as many as 60 whites and 120 Indians gathered to hear Kirkland preach in English and in the Indian languages.

Kirkland's home and the Hamilton-Oneida Academy he founded in 1793 were meeting places for Indians and whites, even after his death in 1808. His grave and that of his Oneida Chief friend Skenondon lie side by side on the campus of Hamilton College in Clinton, New York, the school that has grown from the roots of Kirkland's original academy.